AF304902

# UFO Drawings From The National Archives

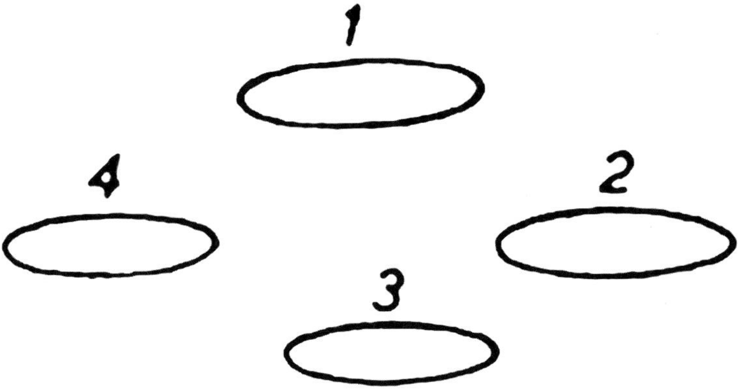



N.B.: – *object 1 appeared first, then 2, then 3, and then 4.*

# UFO Drawings From The National Archives

*David Clarke*

*Four Corners Irregulars*

N⁰ 2

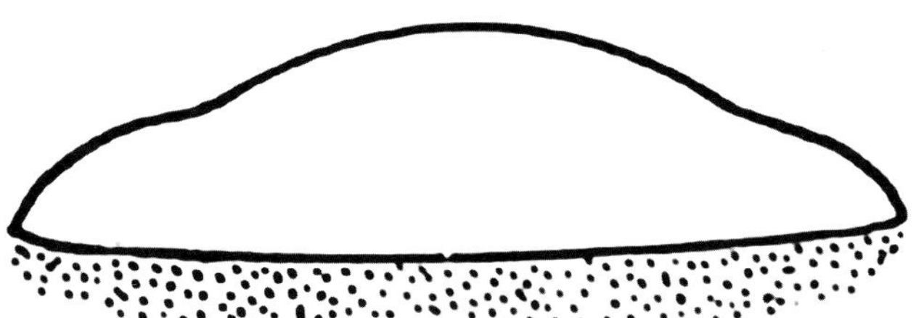

# The Truth Is In Here

## *David Clarke*

From its origins in the aftermath of the Second World War, belief in extra-terrestrial visitations has grown into one of the most widespread and persistent of modern mysteries. As one measure of its impact on British society, a 1998 opinion survey by ICM for the *Daily Mail* found that one third of the UK's population believed that 'extra-terrestrial life has already visited Earth'. Of these, 2 % (1.26 million people) claim to have seen a UFO or had direct experience of alien visitation[1].

In conspiracy culture, stories circulate telling of UFO crashes, government cover-ups and secret agreements between the US military and alien intelligences. In the UK some believe the MoD operate a 'secret army against the aliens' and employ special agents – the legendary Men in Black or MIB – to silence witnesses and remove hard evidence of UFO visitations. But in 2007, after decades of stonewalling questions about its UFO investigations, the MoD announced that it had decided to proactively release all its surviving files. This was, it said, to counter 'the maze of rumour and frequently ill-informed speculation' that surrounded their role in this subject. In recognition of the fact there *was* public interest in the content of their archives, thousands of pages of formerly secret documents were scanned and uploaded to the internet. Only a small amount of information was 'redacted' to remove names and addresses of people who had reported sightings and, occasionally, secret information that might harm national security if released.

The opening of these formerly secret files was a personal victory for me. For a decade before the MoD's announcement I had waged a long campaign, using new powers under Britain's Freedom of Information Act (FOI), for the full disclosure of Britain's UFO files. From 2005, when the act came into force, I used a series of targeted FOI requests under the new act to persuade the Ministry of Defence to make their UFO material available for academic researchers. I argued there was a genuine public interest in how the government had investigated sightings of mysterious objects in the sky and that, by embracing greater openness, they could dispel many misconceptions about a subject long mired in unnecessary secrecy.

I soon found myself swapping the role of poacher for that of a gamekeeper. In 2008 I was offered the opportunity to act as a consultant for The National Archives project that would oversee the release of this enormous collection of records. This project took almost a decade to complete and, when it finally ended in 2017, 227 files containing more than 60,000 pages of correspondence, reports and illustrations were opened via a website created by The National Archives: (nationalarchives.gov.uk/ufos). And that was not all. There is another collection of older UFO files that had already been opened at The National Archives in Kew, southwest London, under the 30 year rule that covers the release of all government records. Some of these date back to the early years of the 20th century. When these two sets of records were combined it produced the largest collection of accounts that describe extraordinary personal experiences in the UK, outside the archives of the Society for Psychical Research at the University of Cambridge.

Since May 2008, when the first of 11 tranches of UFO documents were released online, the project website has received more than 3.7 million visitors from 160 countries. Mass media coverage brought news of the files to an estimated global audience of 25 million people.

The files contain unsorted, and – in the more recent papers – anonymised, accounts of sightings reported to the Ministry of Defence, the RAF, police forces and other authorities since the end of World War 2. Mixed up among the formal and often dry briefings, reports and exchanges between civil servants and politicians are examples of the stories, personal experiences, rumours, beliefs, hopes and fears expressed by British people from all walks of life. Chronologically, the modern UFO files cover an eventful period of sixty years, bookending the world-changing events that marked the beginning and end of the Cold War.

Long ago the MoD had decided these papers were of no 'defence interest'. But I believe they provide a unique insight into aspects of 20th century social history that are often ignored by scholars. Esoteric beliefs and uncanny experiences with UFOs and other mysterious aerial phenomena are the subject of deep interest and fascination for millions of people across the world who, driven by a mixture of curiosity, personal interest and a desire to know 'the truth', continue to visit the online archive to view and download each of the 11 tranches of UFO files.

It is the imaginative artwork of those who see UFOs – and their personal stories – that form the basis of this book. I have scoured the files in search of drawings, paintings and other illustrations in order to produce a visual record of the mysterious phenomena that people have seen and reported to the British government. Occasionally the files contain photographic images allegedly showing UFOs that have been sent to MoD for analysis and explanation. I have included a small number of the more iconic photographs in recognition of the fact they have themselves inspired artists' impressions and even more imaginative interpretations in books and films.


*Opening Britain's UFO Files*

*'What does all this stuff about flying saucers amount to?'*
Winston Churchill asked his advisors in July 1952.

*'What can it mean? What is the truth?'*[2]

In the immediate aftermath of the Second World War, the 77-year-old Prime Minister's feelings of wonder were tinged with an element of apprehension in the face of a potential new threat from the sky. Churchill's curiosity had been piqued by a series of alarming news headlines. For a period of ten days during the summer, anomalous lights and objects had invaded the skies above Washington DC. Alarm bells were set ringing in air traffic control centres across the USA and the concern shared by the CIA and President Truman quickly spread across the Atlantic. The US Air Force scrambled its fastest fighter jets to intercept these intruders. But the 'unexplained blips' easily outpaced them. It was the height of the Cold War and nervous fingers were poised above buttons that could, at any moment, have triggered the Third World War. Churchill's demand to know 'the truth' about flying saucers reflects the questions of many others who, since those days, have seen something unexpected and extraordinary in the sky – or on the ground – and wanted to know: 'What can it mean?'

At times of anxiety, fear and technological change people turn to scientists and military leaders for answers. Hidden beneath layers of Cold War secrecy, experts had already ruled out the possibility these intruding 'objects' could be of Soviet origin. Their observed speed, manoeuvrability and technological performance far exceeded any type of jet aircraft developed on Earth. But the US Air Force and CIA shied away from the idea they might be craft piloted by 'men from Mars'. At a press conference, the air force moved to calm the nerves of a jittery nation. The director of intelligence, Major General John Samford, told the assembled reporters the radar blips were temperature inversions caused by the hot summer weather[3].

The press called these mysterious phenomena 'flying saucers'. But the US Air Force chose a simple acronym: UFOs. The 'Unidentified' in UFO simply means a phenomenon in the sky that *cannot immediately* be identified. The military authorities knew that most sightings turned out, on investigation, to have ordinary explanations. Aircraft, stray balloons, flocks of birds, meteors, bright stars or planets and unusual weather were the most common explanations for UFOs according to the USAF's UFO investigation unit, Project Blue Book. But there were always a few intriguing incidents, including many reports by aircrew and reliable observers such as police officers, that defied the best attempts to explain them away.

During the Cold War the military intelligence agencies in the US and UK were naturally interested in any 'unidentified' objects – such as aircraft, missiles and satellites – that might have a hammer and sickle painted on their fuselage. But for those whose imagination had been stoked by science fiction and comic-book images that depicted spaceships, bug-eyed monsters and Michael Rennie-type visitors from other worlds, there could be only one explanation for UFOs. Presciently, almost one year before the Washington 'flap' a fictional invasion of the US capitol had been predicted in the movie *The Day the Earth Stood Still*. In the opening scene a military radar operator exclaims:

*'...Holy Mackerel! Get the Lieutenant! That thing's doing 4,000! That can't be an aircraft! Must be a buzz bomb! I have a bogey at two zero zero thousand feet, four zero zero zero miles an hour...'*

Flying saucers first arrived in the public consciousness on 24 June 1947 when a private pilot, Kenneth Arnold, spotted 'nine peculiar looking aircraft' soaring in formation near Mount Rainier, in Washington state, at a speed he calculated as being twice that of the most advanced jet aircraft of the day. One of Arnold's first ideas was that he had seen a flight of secret prototype aircraft. His remarkable experience, widely reported by the news media, triggered a wave of similar observations across North America and the world. Two weeks later there were reports that one of the 'flying discs' had crashed on a remote ranch near the Roswell Army Air Force base in New Mexico. But hopes that the mystery would be solved were quickly dashed, when the US Army Air Force announced the 'disc' was a lowly weather balloon.

Ever since those months in 1947, as journalist Bryan Appleyard put it, 'aliens have poured from the abyss that lies between ourselves and the world'[4]. The appearance of flying saucers in great numbers, so soon after our use of atomic weapons in 1945, convinced many people that advanced extra-terrestrial civilisations had long been observing the Earth, much as H.G. Wells had predicted in his 1898 novel *War of the Worlds*. But whilst Wells's Martians were bent on invasion and conquest, the elusive behaviour of the saucers suggested their operators may have benevolent motivations towards human beings. Were they alien anthropologists, watching a primitive species but not interfering? Or were they concerned that we might use our nuclear arsenal to destroy not only ourselves but also endanger our cosmic neighbours?

These ideas were not confined purely to dreamers or readers of comic books. Two years before the Washington UFO 'flap' one of Britain's most decorated military officials, Admiral of the Fleet, Lord Louis Mountbatten, made a startling confession to his friend, Charles Eade, who edited the London *Sunday Dispatch*. Under the condition that his identity was protected, Mountbatten confessed he was convinced flying saucers existed. 'They are not of human agency, that is to say they do not come from our Earth,' he wrote to Eade. 'Maybe it is the Shackletons or Scotts of Venus or Mars who are making the first exploration of our Earth.' Mountbatten's statement exploded as a page one headline in the *Sunday Dispatch* in October 1950[5]. It launched a high-profile series on flying saucers that Eade billed as: 'The story that may be bigger even than atom bomb wars... the No. 1 sensation of the age'.

As a future Chief of Defence Staff, Mountbatten had access to Top Secret material and contacts in the highest levels of the US military. Yet despite this very public, if anonymous, endorsement from a respected figure, when Winston Churchill demanded to 'know the truth', he was told flying saucers were an American fad. The government's chief scientific advisor, Sir John Cockcroft, described them as 'a product of mass psychology'. But the Air Staff admitted that a secret intelligence study of unusual sightings had been completed by a 'Flying Saucer Working Party' reporting to the Ministry of Defence in 1951. This had concluded that all incidents reported to date, in the UK at least, could be explained as misperceptions of natural and man-made phenomena, hallucinations and deliberate hoaxes.

The more exciting possibility that *some* UFOs could be interplanetary visitors was ruled out in one scathing paragraph: 'When the only material available is a mass of purely subjective evidence it is impossible to give anything like scientific proof that the phenomena observed are, or are not, caused by something entirely novel, such as aircraft of extra-terrestrial origin, developed by beings unknown to us on lines more advanced than anything we have thought of'[6].

Impossible or not, later in the same year that Churchill was reassured there was nothing to worry about, it was time for members of the Royal Air Force to observe wonders in the sky. On a bright, sunny afternoon in September 1952, Flight Lieutenant John Kilburn was standing on the airfield at RAF Topcliffe in North Yorkshire, alongside a group of Shackleton aircrew from 269 squadron. They were among 80,000 military personnel from eight countries who were part of a massive NATO exercise, code-named Mainbrace, that was to simulate a Soviet attack on the west. Gazing skywards, Kilburn spotted a Meteor jet approaching the airfield at 5,000 feet. Then one of his colleagues noticed something extraordinary: a silver circular object much higher in the sky that appeared to be following the Meteor. Initially the men thought a parachute or piece of engine cowling had detached itself from the aircraft. But then, suddenly, the object descended 'swinging in a pendular motion… similar to a falling sycamore leaf' towards the jet. It began rotating on its own axis, before it accelerated away to the west at a speed 'in excess of that that of a shooting star'.

'I have never seen such a phenomenon before,' Kilburn reported. 'The movements of the object were not identifiable with anything I have seen in the air and the rate of acceleration was unbelievable'[7]. His one-page statement has taken its place among the documents at The National Archives. It was one of the first accounts of an unexplained sighting to be entered into the government's records. But in 1952 there was no British organisation, squirrelled away in the heart of Whitehall, responsible for UFOs.

That was soon to change. A copy of the signal reporting Kilburn's sighting reached the office of the Vice Chief of the Air Staff, Sir Ralph Cochrane, where it was seen by a civil servant called Ralph Noyes. Decades later, when the Topcliffe papers were opened at The National Archives, Noyes – who had retired as an Under Secretary of State – recalled his own 'embarrassed unease' shared, he said by colleagues in the Air Ministry, that 'our own people had begun to fall for that saucer nonsense'. Someone in Noyes' office scribbled a casual instruction in the margin of the report: 'Unidentified aircraft or objects... Ask PA [personal assistant] to open Folder'.

'Clearly no folder, still less an official file, had yet been opened by the Operations staff on flying saucers,' at that point, Noyes recalled[8].

There were several false starts before the British government recognised that its own armed forces and, increasingly, many of its ordinary citizens, were reporting encounters with unidentified objects in the sky. What should be done about it? The Air Ministry decided this was the moment to create a special UFO investigation unit. It would be the task of its air intelligence staff, working alongside civilian experts in a number of MoD departments, to investigate and, where possible, find rational explanations for those UFOs that refused to go away.

Initially, the Air Ministry's UFO unit was based in an old attic room of the Hotel Metropole, a government building on the corner of Northumberland Avenue and Whitehall, in central London. It was led by an Ulster-born RAF Wing Commander, Myles Formby, who had served on the MoD's Flying Saucer Working Party. Towards the end of the war Formby examined and test-flew captured German aircraft, including futuristic designs that resembled some of the flying saucers that had been reported. But Formby's tiny unit never had the formal status, staff or financial support enjoyed by its US counterpart Project Blue Book.

To make sense of the stories flowing into the UFO unit, the Air Ministry devised a system to record, categorise and analyse the data it collected. In 1953 orders were circulated to RAF and Royal Navy stations demanding that all military personnel should report any 'unusual sightings' through official channels to Air Ministry. Under no circumstances, it said, should they speak to the press about their sightings unless authorised to do so by the ministry[9].

Secondly, a questionnaire was created to record details of sightings reported by members of the armed forces and the public. Each year the Air Ministry received hundreds of letters and phone calls from ordinary people who wished to report their sightings. Some of these arrived via the police, coastguard or civil aviation authority. Those who left a contact address were asked to complete a version of the form that was used by Project Blue Book staff, in the USA, to collect basic data. The form included a series of questions, including the observer/s name and address, the date, time and location of their sighting and the height, speed, shape, size, colour and position in the sky of the phenomena they had observed. Updated versions of this questionnaire were still used by the MoD in 2009. This type of information was essential as it provided clues that could help officials to evaluate and categorise sightings into a list of explanatory categories.

From its creation the Air Ministry's UFO unit operated under the cover of an intelligence branch known as DDI (Tech), reflecting the British establishment's obsession with secrecy. This was partly because it wished to avoid the attention of the press who saw flying saucers as a source of easy, sensational copy. John Kilburn's sighting was exceptional because it was made by a 'credible witness' – a member of His Majesty's armed forces. Such stories tended to make news headlines but in the context of the files, they were few and far between. In stark contrast the majority of reports came from civilians. As one official put it: 'of 570 witnesses 447 were school children, 51 were housewives and 18 were policemen. There were 49 other occupations, none of them providing more than eight witnesses'. This breakdown 'told its own story', the official added, 'but I am not sure how best to get it across'[10].

There was also a new category of observer, the UFOlogist, who went looking for UFOs and was keen to report them to the Air Ministry. In 1952 the first club for UFO enthusiasts, The British Flying Saucer Bureau, was established in Bristol by Captain Edward Plunkett, a retired merchant mariner. Its self-appointed remit was to investigate and disseminate news about the latest sightings. Three years later the first international magazine devoted to UFOs, *Flying Saucer Review*, was launched in London. Published bi-monthly, in its first year FSR was edited by a retired Battle of Britain fighter pilot, Derek Dempster.

As public fascination for UFOs increased, so did questions from the press and, occasionally, from MPs in House of Commons. Even worse, from the ministry's point of view, was the sheer number of UFOlogists, amateur experts and the type of person that broadcaster Patrick Moore, a veteran UFO sceptic, called 'independent thinkers'. These were people who, frustrated by the lack of official confirmation that flying saucers existed, organised letter-writing campaigns that demanded – much as

Churchill had – 'the truth'. When answers were not forthcoming the more paranoid saucerers began to suspect a gigantic government cover-up was under way.

Some UFO enthusiasts tried to apply the scientific method to the study of these phenomena. Others abandoned science altogether and saw flying saucers as symbols of a new religious movement. The best known British example was a society launched by a London taxi-driver and anti-nuclear activist turned cosmic avatar, George King, from his Maida Vale flat. From 1954, King began channelling spirit messages from what he claimed were highly-advanced alien intelligences based on Mars, Venus and Saturn. His main telepathic contact, whom he called 'Aetherius', warned that Earth was in danger of destruction if our experimentation with nuclear weapons continued. According to King, flying saucers were one of the signs used by cosmic masters to warn us of the dangers we faced. In 1958 members of King's society staged a demonstration outside the Air Ministry building in London, demanding an end to official secrecy about UFOS. It was to be the first of many campaigns for disclosure of UFO information that have left an imprint upon the MoD records.

Soon afterwards, a decision was taken that all public statements on UFOS would, in future, be handled not by the RAF or military officials, but by civil servants working in the Air Staff secretariat[11]. This administrative shake-up led to the creation of what would become popularly known as the 'UFO desk'. This was the focal point in the MoD where all reports of mysterious sightings ended up, before they were sent for analysis or investigation by air defence specialists. The first UFO desk officer was based in a civilian branch of the MoD known as S6 (Air). Later the responsibility for UFOS was shared with a sister branch, S4 (Air), that handled public relations issues for the RAF. After the creation of the unified Ministry of Defence from 1960, the name of this branch changed frequently, but essentially it remained the focal point for all UFO reports that reached Whitehall.

S6's first UFO desk officer, David West, joined the Air Ministry as a trainee clerk in 1946 on leaving school. A decade later, whilst he and colleagues were preoccupied with the Suez crisis, he began drafting answers to Parliamentary questions from Members of Parliament about flying saucer sightings. In his responses to letters from members of the public, West established the tone of bored detachment that would become a characteristic feature of statements made by the UFO desk during the half century that followed. For example, in 1958 he informed colleagues that 'for the most part we expect to be politely unhelpful' when asked what MoD knew about UFOS[12].

Despite an influx of letters and questions from the press, public interest in UFOs at this time was deemed to be low and, in the absence of a Freedom of Information Act, many records created by the UFO desk were destroyed. This was because officials decided they contained 'nothing of defence interest'. The policy was justified on the grounds that because so many of the UFO reports were found to have mundane explanations the ministry could see no purpose in retaining them for release to the public after the usual 30 years, as was the system for other government files, under 1958 Public Records Act. It was not until the mid-1990s, when the US-made television series *The X-Files* became a household name, that serious pressure was placed on the MoD to be more open about what their own UFO investigations had discovered. When some of the earlier surviving UFO files were finally opened to the public, from 1994, they were largely a disappointment to those who hoped they might contain hard evidence of extra-terrestrial visitations to Britain. Instead, the records revealed how the MoD was able to identify – at least to the satisfaction of the UFO desk staff – most of the sightings reported to them, without recourse to more exotic theories. This was achieved by categorising sightings as observations of natural and man-made phenomena that, experience had demonstrated, were often misperceived as something *extra*-ordinary. These included conventional civilian aircraft 'viewed from unaccustomed angles' and military jet aircraft 'flying at great speeds and heights, mistaken by untrained and, at times, trained observers'; sunlight reflections from aircraft and balloons and of car headlights on low cloud; meteorological balloons, bright meteors and fireballs. As the Space Race grew in pace with the Soviet Union's successful launch of the first satellite, Sputnik, in 1957 man-made satellites and space junk added to the growing catalogue of common sources for UFO reports. Other culprits included bright stars and planets prominent in the night sky at certain times of year, birds and unusual cloud formations. Privately, some officials suspected extremely rare natural phenomena, such as atmospheric plasmas not yet recognised by science, may be responsible for some of the more impressive observations reported by military and civilian aircrew.

UFO desk officers could call upon a range of scientific and military expertise to assist in their inquiries. These included the Meteorological Office, the Royal Greenwich Observatory and specialist RAF staff who had access to data from powerful radars that scanned the UK air defence region for evidence of enemy aircraft. Until 2000 the UFO desk copied details of sightings it received to a secretive branch of the Defence Intelligence

Staff, DI55, who were responsible for monitoring ballistic missiles and satellites launched by foreign powers. But DI55 admitted that because the vast majority of sightings could be explained as 'satellites, space debris, rocket launches or manifestations of meteorological or other natural phenomena', they were given a very low priority. One DI55 desk officer, in response to a request from the *Daily Mirror* for a briefing on UFOs by the MoD, responded: '[we] regularly receive reports... but we can do little other than scan through them and file. They do provide the occasional flash of (unintentional) humour to brighten our lives. Very occasionally they pose an interesting puzzle which we cannot follow up'[13].

Another DI55 desk officer, when asked about the possibility that some UFOs could be extra-terrestrial visitors, questioned why aliens would wish to visit 'an insignificant planet (the Earth) of an insignificant star (the sun)'. Even if intelligent aliens existed, he opined, the Earth should expect a visit perhaps once in every thousand years, so 'claims of thousands of visits in the last decade... are far too large to be credible'[14]. Others were more optimistic and, to use a popular phrase from *The X-Files*, 'wanted to believe'. For example, in 1995 a DI55 officer, in a briefing paper prepared for MoD, said that if some UFOs were alien visitations then the motivation for their visits might include 'military reconnaissance, scientific, tourism'[15].

This type of blue sky thinking occurs infrequently in the files. As journalist Chris Wright observed, 'it seems astonishing that one of the most enduring mysteries of modern times should be reduced to a flurry of stolid paperwork'[16]. Much of the UFO desk officers' time was spent sifting through press cuttings and letters received from ordinary folk who wanted to tell *someone* about their extraordinary experiences. Many letter-writers had an apologetic tone, conveying the writer's own sense of incredulity, puzzlement and occasionally fear. A typical comment is: 'I do not believe in "little green men" nor in flying saucers, but... I have never before seen anything like them and incidentally, I am a teetotaller'[17]. Another common feature of letters is a fear of ridicule from friends and colleagues if their stories were released publicly or, even worse, that they might be regarded as suffering from hallucinations. One survey of UFO spotters in 1968 found that 87% of those surveyed had reported their sighting only to immediate family and friends[18]. Those who decided to make a formal statement to the police or MoD were, in fact, a tiny minority of the total number of UFO witnesses.

The files reveal how the vast majority of UFO witnesses are not obsessive enthusiasts, or fantasists, but ordinary people who sincerely believed they have seen something truly extraordinary in the sky. As concerned citizens, they felt it was their public duty to report their experiences to someone in authority. In the absence of any recognised scientific body with an interest in the subject, the police or MoD became their default choice. Most wanted to report 'lights in the sky' or anomalous objects they spotted fleetingly and unexpectedly. In a minority of cases the experiences could be life-changing. Some reported feelings of fear and terror. For example a Lancashire woman wrote to the MoD in 1988 reporting how she had inexplicably lost one hour of a journey in which she, and her mother, had been buzzed by a huge and dazzlingly-bright object 'roughly about the size of a double-decker bus on its side'. Afterwards the woman suffered nightmares and discovered puzzling bruises on her legs. 'Please,' she pleaded in her letter, 'could you help me to solve or at least explain... what happened on that road... I can't talk to anyone about this because I don't think most people would believe. But I swear it happened'[19].

When it came to reports of alleged 'alien abductions' the response was often terse and unhelpful. 'Abduction is a criminal offence and as such it is a matter for the civil police,' a desk officer told one inquirer in 1996. 'As the MoD is not aware of any evidence which might substantiate the existence of extraterrestrial activity of the type to which you allude, this is a non-issue as far as the MoD are concerned'[20]. In cases like this officials had few options and no answers. The standard response sent to members of the public reporting UFO experiences was: 'The MoD does not have any expertise or role in respect of UFO/flying saucer matters or to the question of the existence or otherwise of extraterrestrial lifeforms, about which it remains totally open-minded'.

One of the striking omissions from the files is the lack of any unambiguous photographs that show 'flying saucers' or structured craft of unknown origin. Apart from a few iconic – and controversial – images, such as those of the UFO fleet photographed by a schoolboy near Sheffield in 1962 (see pp. 120–122) many photographs submitted to the UFO desk show anomalous images that were not noticed by the photographer at the moment the shutter was pressed. A classic example is the mysterious 'spaceman' (see pp. 36–37) that appears in a photograph taken by a

Cumbrian fireman of his young daughter at a beauty spot overlooking the Solway Coast in Cumbria in 1964[21]. Most anomalous images of this kind turn out, on analysis by qualified experts, to be tricks of the light, either as double-exposures on the film itself or artefacts created by reflections inside the camera lens. On other occasions birds and other natural phenomena have been captured on the camera film but were not noticed by the photographer at the time the image was taken. By the beginning of the 21st century there were hundreds of thousands of amateur still and video images allegedly showing UFOs and aliens. But not a single one provides convincing evidence of alien craft operating either in Earth's skies or in outer space. When you consider the very large number of people who carry sophisticated cameras and the increasing power of digital camera technology on mobile phones, the conspicuous lack of photographic evidence among the 12,000 UFO sightings reported to the MoD since 1952 tells its own story.

In the absence of convincing photographic proof, UFO spotters have turned to pen, pencil, crayons and occasionally even paintbrush in order to convey the full impact of their experiences. In one case a schoolteacher gathered a group of youngsters together and asked them to draw the UFO they had seen from their playground, using paper and coloured crayons. Their images ended up in the UFO files after they were sent by Cheshire Police to the Ministry of Defence[22]. Striking examples of drawings depicting UFOs and alien creatures of all shapes and sizes occur throughout the full chronological sequence of files. Most of the illustrations in this book lack the sophistication of drawings produced by professional artists for use in newspapers and magazines. Viewed from a purely aesthetic viewpoint, sketches of UFOs made by schoolchildren or policemen might appear naïve or worthless. But as visual evidence of unusual sightings that are deeply meaningful and significant to those individuals who see UFOs, they are uniquely valuable historical documents in their own right, and shed light on how the events and popular culture of the age imprinted on people's imaginations.


*The closure of the UFO Desk*


The success of the *The X-Files* TV series and blockbuster films featuring UFOs, such as *Independence Day* released shortly before the 50th anniversary of the Roswell incident, ensured that public fascination for the UFO phenomenon continued to grow. But just as public interest increased, government concern about UFOs as a real or potential threat to defence withered away. Early in 1997 the Ministry of Defence was obliged to set up a telephone answering service to cope with a doubling of its workload on UFOs. In April that year an official complained to his superiors that he was struggling to answer a stream of letters 'from members of the public... seeking information about the existence of alien life forms, or seeking a detailed investigation/explanation for allegations of abduction by aliens, out of the body experiences, animal mutilations, crop circles, etc'[23].

Letters and emails poured into the ministry's inbox, many addressed to MPs and to the new Labour Prime Minister, Tony Blair, who had pledged to introduce a Freedom of Information Act. After his success, UFO aficionados appealed to him to 'consider making available for public scrutiny all of the many and varied UFO reports compiled by the government'. Behind the scenes, the Ministry of Defence was keen to draw a line under almost 60 years of its involvement in the UFO controversy. 'The sole interest of the MoD in UFO reports is to establish whether they reveal anything of defence interest,' read the UFO desk's terms of reference. But after examining some 12,000 sighting reports received since the 1950s no evidence of a defence threat posed by UFOs had been identified. With cuts to defence expenditure adding to the growing cost of fighting two expensive ground wars in Afghanistan and Iraq, it was difficult for ministers to justify spending scarce resources on a UFO hotline. The MoD's declining interest in the subject led the space intelligence branch DI55 who had, for fifty years, secretly monitored the more interesting reports, to notify the UFO desk it no longer needed access to information on the latest sightings. The UFO hotline simply encouraged members of the public, including many UFO enthusiasts, to report stories that were then placed on file, encouraging others like myself to make FOI requests to see them.

In a report on the daily mechanics of what was, undoubtedly, one of the strangest jobs in Whitehall, UFO desk officer Paul Webb poured cold water on the popular idea that MoD operated a lavishly-funded secret 'UFO project'. In 2007 Webb wrote that the very idea of official investigations 'tends to suggest... there are Top Secret teams of specialist scientists scurrying around the country in a real life version of the X-Files'. Striking what sounds like a note of disappointment, he admitted this was 'total fiction' and most of his investigations were carried out simply by 'googling the internet'[24].

The closure of Britain's X-Files was inevitable. In November 2009 Defence Minister Bob Ainsworth was advised that MoD wanted 'to reduce very significantly the UFO task which is consuming increasing resource, but produces no valuable defence output'. Ainsworth was told that, in more than 50 years, 'no UFO sighting reported to [MoD] has ever revealed anything to suggest an extra-terrestrial presence or military threat to the UK [and] there is no defence benefit in [MoD] recording, collating, analysing or investigating UFO sightings'[25].

Paul Webb took a more nuanced view of the closure decision. In a valedictory email dated 2 June 2009 he told his superiors it was 'fair to say that the release programme itself... has been a success for the MoD'. Naturally, he said, the press 'tend to concentrate on the more sensational stories (especially those with drawings of aliens!) but I believe that despite the predicted increased interest in the subject in the short term, the wider general public is starting to get a more accurate impression of our role in UFO matters'[26].


1. *Daily Mail*, 2 February 1998.
2. PREM 11/855
3. USAF press conference 24 July 1952: https://www.youtube.com/watch?v=bAGZQT8FSPk
4. Appleyard, B. *Aliens: Why they are here*, Scribner 2005.
5. *Sunday Dispatch*, 1 October 1950
6. DEFE 44/119
7. AIR 16/1199
8. Ralph Noyes, 'The Magical Mystery Tour', *Magonia* 29, April 1988.
9. AIR 2/9994
10. DEFE 24/3152
11. DEFE 31/118
12. Op. cit
13. DEFE 24/1517
14. AIR 20/12966
15. DEFE 24/2080/1
16. Chris Wright, 'From the annals of Britain's UFO Desk', *The Boston Globe*, 26 August 2012.
17. AIR 20/11890
18. Greg Eghigian, 'Making UFOs make sense: UFOlogy, science, and the history of their mutual distrust,' *Public Understanding of Science*, December 2015.
19. DEFE 24/1929/1
20. DEFE 24/1979/1
21. DEFE 24/1983/1
22. DEFE 24/1206
23. DEFE 24/1986/1
24. DEFE 24/2087/1
25. DEFE 24/2458/1
26. DEFE 24/2458/1

*next spread* —▷

## UFO shapes

The Ministry of Defence files contain details of 11,000 sightings reported between 1962 and 2009 when the UFO desk and its telephone hotline were closed. On average, desk officers logged between 100–200 accounts each year but sometimes, as in 1978 following the release of the movie *Close Encounters of the Third Kind*, the numbers doubled or trebled. Descriptions in the files are incredibly varied. They include the classic flat disc-shaped flying saucer, sometimes with a dome or domes, circular, ellipsoid or egg-shaped objects, cigar-shaped and cylindrical UFOs. Since the 1980s, one of the most popular shapes has been the delta-winged or triangular-shaped objects that reflect the sleak design of the USAF Stealth fighter and B2 bomber. Other UFO shapes include cone-shaped, pyramidal, crescent and ring-shaped. In 1971 the Oxford-based UFO group Contact UK produced a report that acknowledged the 'almost bewildering variety' of UFO shapes. One conclusion was that no two UFOs are identical. Contact preferred to believe that 'despite various apparent differences in detail' most UFOs 'can be grouped around several distinct basic designs', similar to the products of the human motor vehicle industry! Their report, sent to the MoD, concluded that it was necessary to 'allow for the possibility that two or more quite different races of UFOnauts are currently visiting Earth, that these may emanate from entirely different points in space and/or time, or from different dimensions or orders of matter, and that the numerous recorded differences in UFO designs are the result of this and are to be expected'. AIR 2/19086

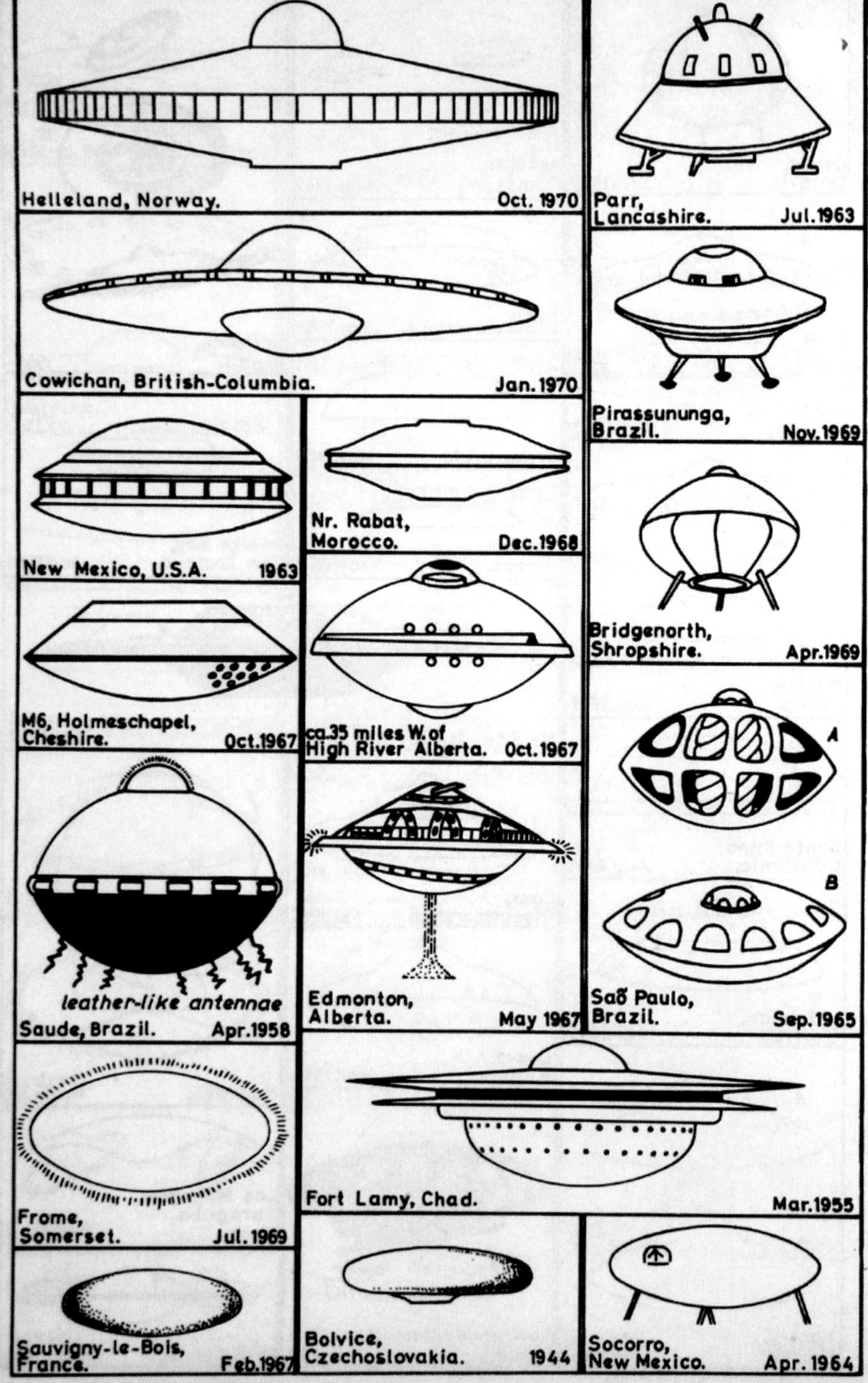
Helleland, Norway.
Oct. 1970
Parr,
Lancashire.
Jul. 1963
Cowichan, British-Columbia.
Jan. 1970
Pirassununga,
Brazil.
Nov. 1969
New Mexico, U.S.A.
1963
Nr. Rabat,
Morocco.
Dec. 1968
Bridgenorth,
Shropshire.
Apr. 1969
M6, Holmeschapel,
Cheshire.
Oct. 1967
ca. 35 miles W. of
High River Alberta.
Oct. 1967
A
leather-like antennae
Saude, Brazil.
Apr. 1958
Edmonton,
Alberta.
May 1967
Saõ Paulo,
Brazil.
Sep. 1965
B
Frome,
Somerset.
Jul. 1969
Fort Lamy, Chad.
Mar. 1955
Sauvigny-le-Bois,
France.
Feb. 1967
Bolvice,
Czechoslovakia.
1944
Socorro,
New Mexico.
Apr. 1964

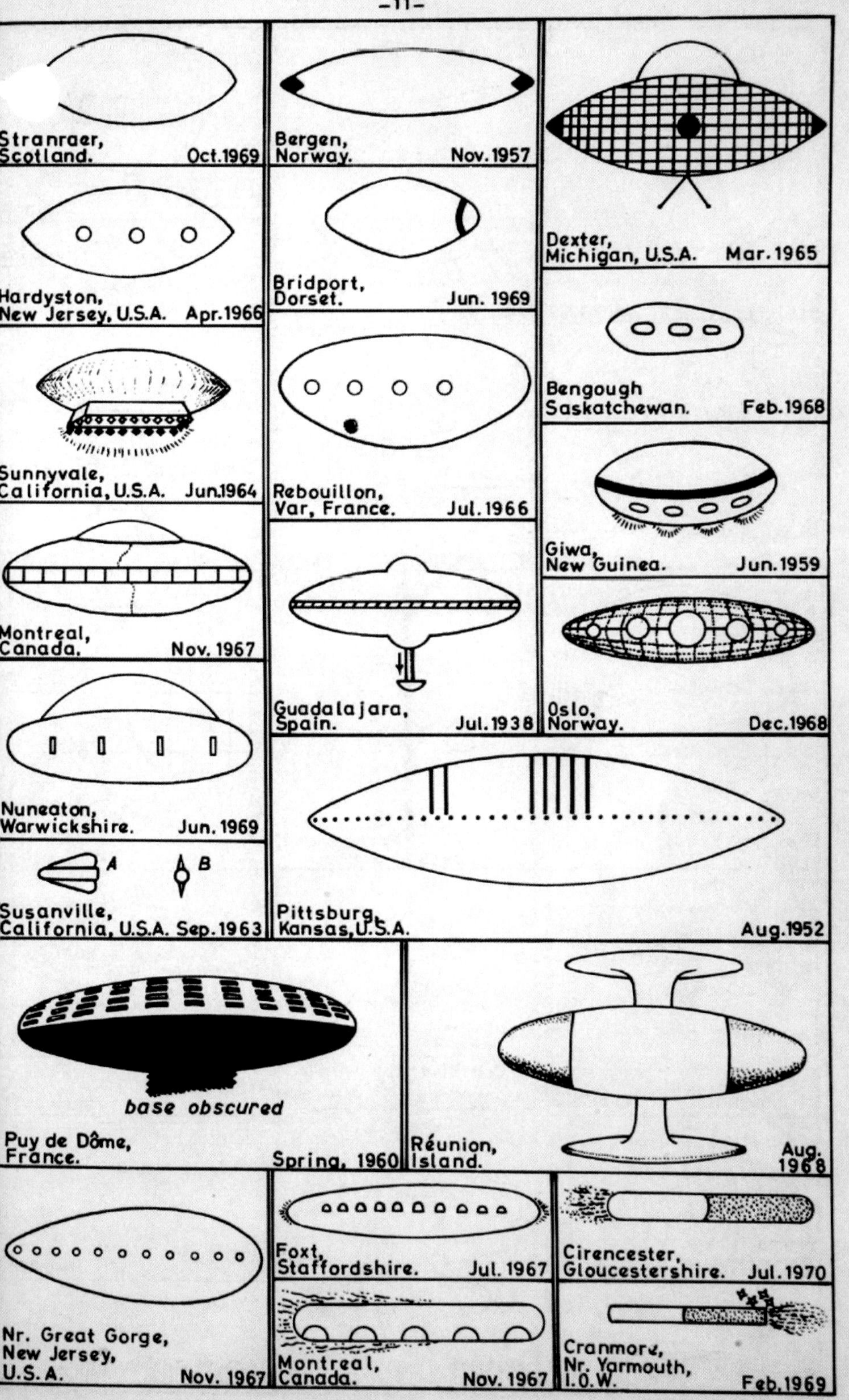
Stranraer, Scotland. Oct.1969
Bergen, Norway. Nov. 1957
Dexter, Michigan, U.S.A. Mar. 1965
Hardyston, New Jersey, U.S.A. Apr.1966
Bridport, Dorset. Jun. 1969
Bengough Saskatchewan. Feb.1968
Sunnyvale, California, U.S.A. Jun.1964
Rebouillon, Var, France. Jul. 1966
Giwa, New Guinea. Jun.1959
Montreal, Canada. Nov. 1967
Guadalajara, Spain. Jul. 1938
Oslo, Norway. Dec.1968
Nuneaton, Warwickshire. Jun. 1969
A
B
Susanville, California, U.S.A. Sep. 1963
Pittsburg, Kansas, U.S.A. Aug.1952
base obscured
Puy de Dôme, France. Spring, 1960
Réunion, Island. Aug. 1968
Nr. Great Gorge, New Jersey, U.S.A. Nov. 1967
Foxt, Staffordshire. Jul. 1967
Montreal, Canada. Nov. 1967
Cirencester, Gloucestershire. Jul. 1970
Cranmore, Nr. Yarmouth, I.O.W. Feb.1969

At the height of the Second World War, in 1940–41, the security service MI5 investigated reports of strange lights in the sky and mysterious 'ground markings' at locations across the British Isles. Before the invasions of France and Norway, so-called fifth columnists had guided German aircraft to targets using signals such as markings in cornfields. Soon after the Battle of Britain, RAF aircrew were asked to look out for 'suspicious patterns laid out on the ground' that might serve as landmarks for Luftwaffe bombers. A number of odd-looking formations, that resembled modern crop circles were reported to MI5 including an 'unusual mark', 33 yards long and in the form of a letter G, in a field near an ordnance factory in South Wales. When quizzed the farmer explained the marking was created innocently, when he sowed surplus barley across a growing field of wheat. In a report completed in 1942 Guy Liddell, MI5's head of counter-espionage, said they had investigated hundreds of similar reports but found no evidence of any fifth column operating in Britain. KV 4/11

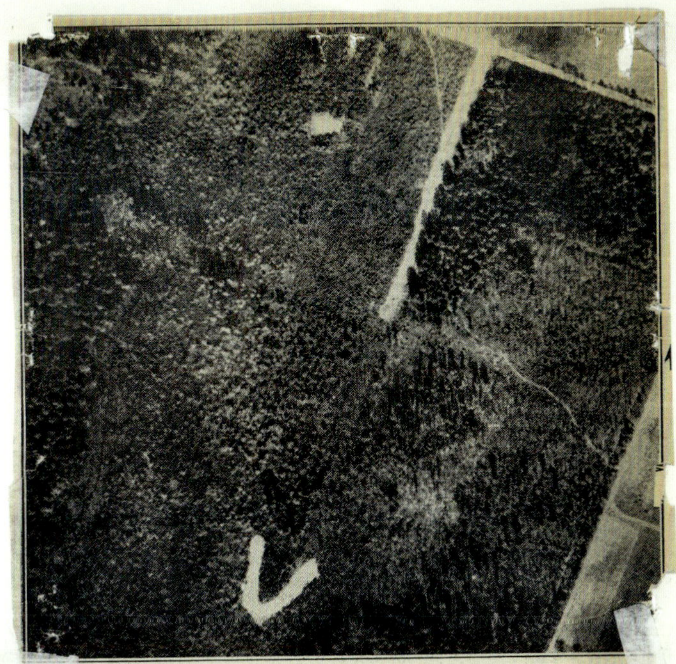

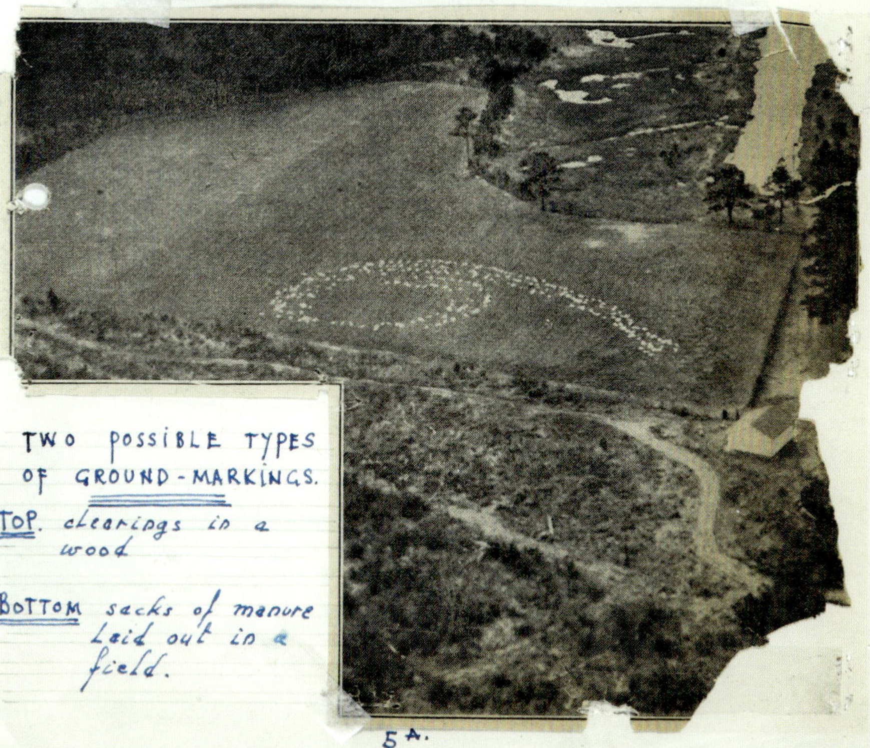

TWO POSSIBLE TYPES
OF GROUND-MARKINGS.

TOP. clearings in a
wood

BOTTOM sacks of manure
laid out in a
field.

5A.

1.    Field at Little Mill, Monmouthshire.

          In May 1941 a report was made that an unusual mark was
visible amongst the growing corn.   Near one of the gates was a
mark in the form of the letter 'G', some 33 yards long.  (See
photograph)  This mark had been made by sowing barley transversely
through the grain.   Air photographs were taken and it was seen
that the tail of the marking pointed towards the Ordnance factory
at Glascoed.

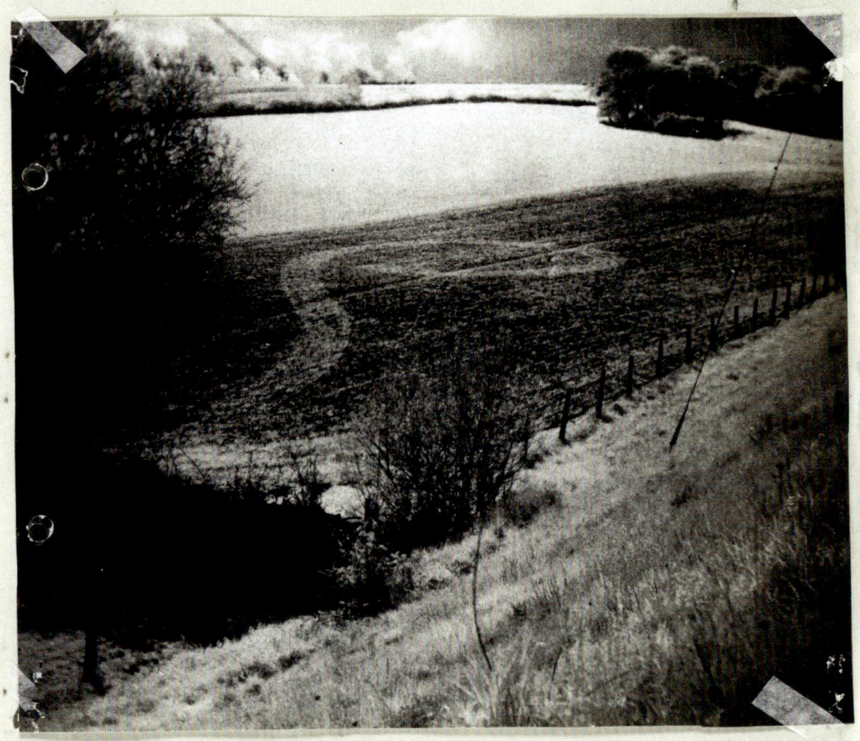

The farmer, a man of good character, was interviewed, and admitted
that he had sown the field himself.   He explained that he had
sold the field in April.   Shortly after, having a drilling machine
nearby which had a small quantity of barley seed in it, and
wishing to empty it as he had to return it to the farmer from whom
he had borrowed it that night, he turned his team of horses into

*next spread* —▷

## 1944

During the Second World War, USAF aircrew coined the phrase 'foo fighters' to describe mysterious lights that pursued their aircraft during night-time raids over occupied Europe. Lights and 'guided rockets' that paced aircraft in a controlled, seemingly intelligent manner were also reported by RAF bomber crews who initially believed they were advanced German secret weapons. One of the most detailed first-hand accounts of a WW2 encounter was recalled by 90-year-old Ronald Claridge DFC AEA in a letter to the MP Tam Dalyell in 2003. Ron became an amateur artist in his retirement and produced a stunning watercolour painting of the object he and eight other members of his Lancaster crew saw one night in the summer of 1944. He was the radio operator in the bomber, commanded by Brian Frow, then aged 21, flight commander of No 7 Pathfinder Squadron. On the night of 11 August they were returning from a raid on oil-refineries in southern France at 25,000 feet when the radar malfunctioned and Frow called out 'What the hell is that?' Moving into the astrodome for a better view, Claridge saw 'an enormous string of lights, on course with us at about a distance of one thousand yards'. The lights, 'like portholes on a ship', appeared to be the edge of an enormous disc-shaped object. The crew were stunned into silence but, 50 years later, Claridge could still remember 'a feeling of complete calm and happiness' that pervaded the aircraft, 'so that even our gunners who would normally open fire were helpless'. After three minutes it suddenly shot ahead and was gone, leaving no noise, vapour or turbulence in its wake. On return to RAF Oakington they were debriefed by RAF intelligence and told not to discuss the incident or put anything in their logbooks. 'But the technology we saw and reported, by all eight of us, was way beyond anything which could be conceived even today'. personal communication, 2003; AIR 14/2076

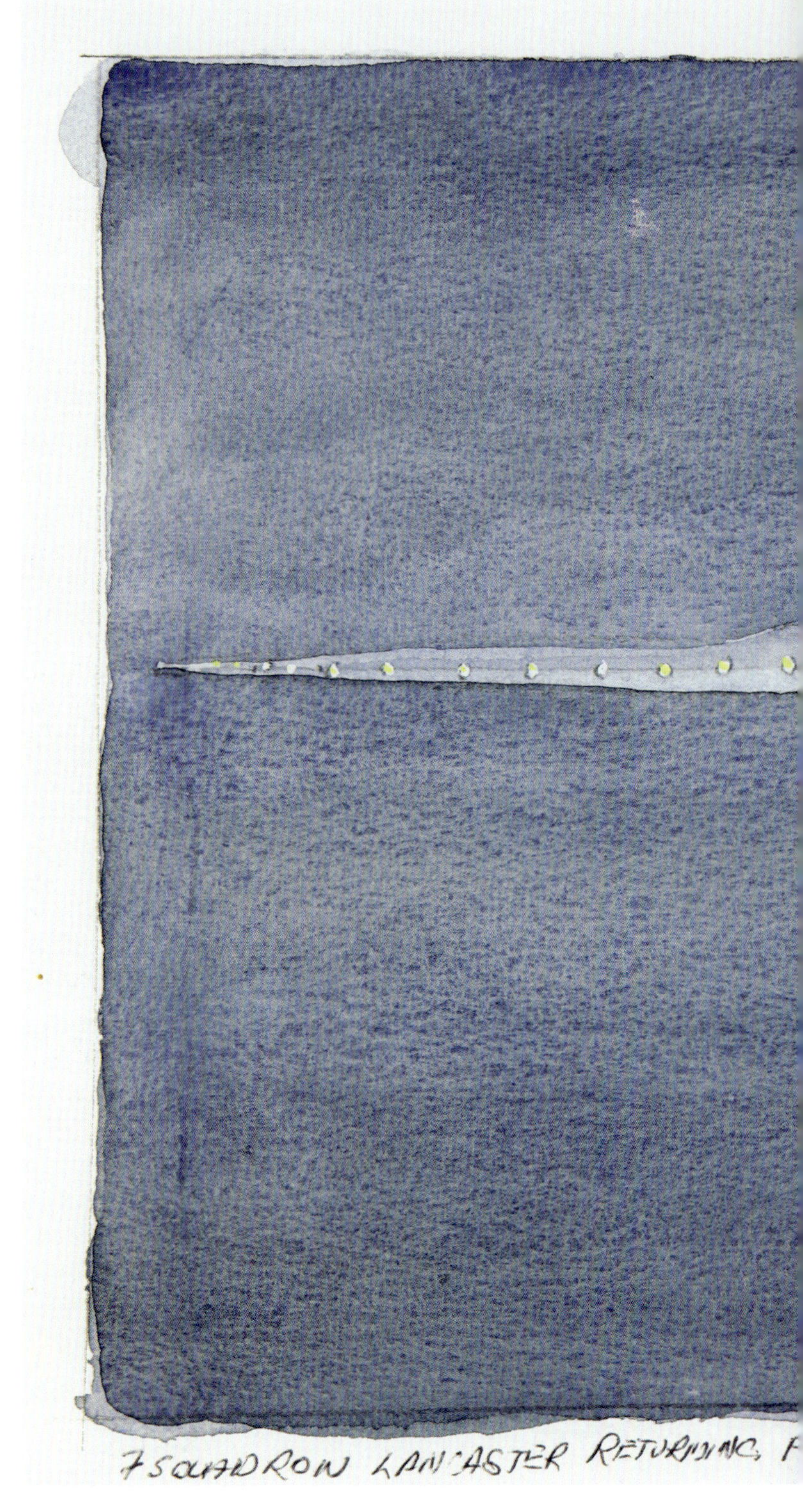

7 SQUADRON LANCASTER RETURNING F

...MBING OIL REFINERY La PALICE FRANCE 11.8.44 MASTER BOMBER

2 MATT BLACK 'UFOs' SIGHTED PASSING OVER BREWERY YARD
CAPE HILL SMETHWICK   SEP. 1964.
MON. 1-15 PM

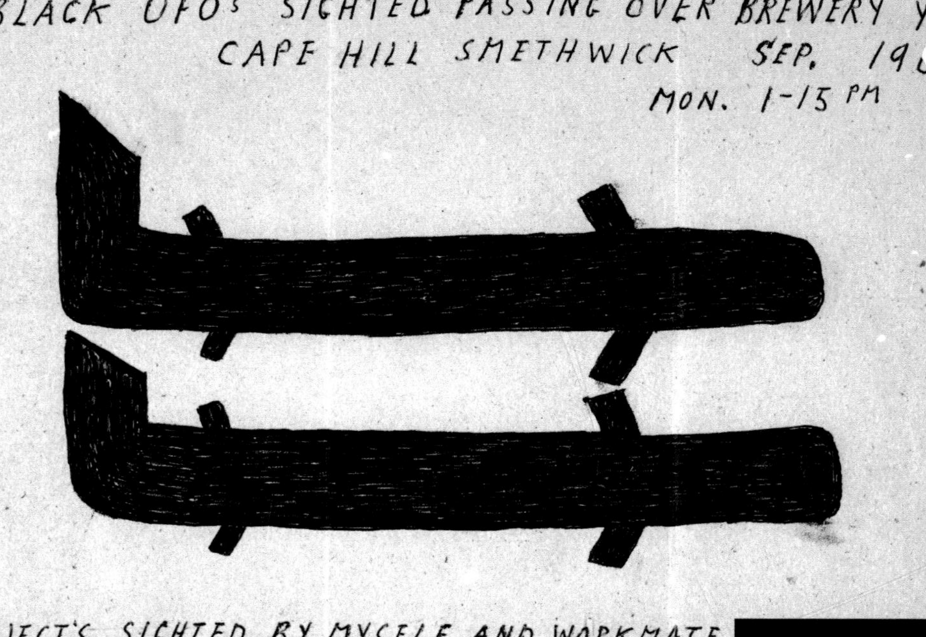

THESE 2 OBJECT'S SIGHTED BY MYSELF AND WORKMATE
APPROX. '30FT IN LENGTH, LOOKED LIKE SHARK-MISSILE, MATT BLACK
IN COLOUR, FLEW TOGETHER FRONT FINS ALMOST TOUCHING.
NO INSIGNIA, NO PORTHOLES, NO COCKPIT'S, NO ENGINES,
TOTALLY SILENT.  SPEED 30 MPH AT HEIGHT 40 FT
IN VIEW 10 SEC. LAST SEEN JUST CLEARING OFFICE BLOCK
ON A HEADING TOWARD'S GROVE LANE.

UFO SIGHTED FROM BEDROOM WINDOW 11-50 PM 3RD SAT. AUG. 1954.
SMETHWICK. W. MIDLANDS. WEATHER CONDITIONS HUMID.
OBJECT PASSED APPROX.
12 FT ABOVE ME.
IN SIGHT 2 MIN.
SPEED 5 MPH
3 PORTHOLES?
SHOWING BLUE-WHITE LIGHT
SIMILAR TO WELDING FLASH.
NO INSIGNIA DISPLAYED
LETTERS OR NUMBERS.
AS OBJECT PASSED DIRECTLY
ABOVE ME I NOTED WHAT
LOOKED LIKE MANHOLE COVER
AT BASE OF
CONTROL TOWER 3 FT IN DIA.
FLASHING BLUE LIGHT FIXED,
NOT REVOLVING.
AROUND BASE OF DOME
COIL OF CABLE - WIRE
OBJECT APPEARED
TO BE ALL OF ONE PIECE
AS IF CAST INSTEAD
OF BUILT.
LOOKED LIKE
ALUMINIUM.
MAYBE 30 FT
IN WIDTH.
TOTALLY SILENT.
RELEASING TRAIL OF SMOKE
FROM REAR.

◁— *previous spread*

## 1954

A letter from Warley, West Midlands, addressed to the MoD, dated 9 June 1994: 'Over the past 40 years I have sighted many UFOs all of which I have found both interesting and puzzling... of course over this period of time I have formed an opinion as to the origin of [these] objects'. The letter was accompanied by two drawings, one depicting an object sighted over Smethwick in August 1954 that 'appeared to be all of one piece as if cast instead of built'. The letter added: 'There are others including ball of light objects, one of which gave a fantastic display of speed... but for now I would be obliged if you would study my reports and let me have an answer'. In appearance it resembles the flying saucer 'scoutship' photographed by the Polish-American contactee George Adamski, who claimed to have taken trips to Venus and Saturn as a guest of friendly, angelic aliens in 1952. Images of the Venusian scoutship first appeared in his best-selling 1953 book *Flying Saucers Have Landed*, co-authored with Desmond Leslie. DEFE 24/1967/1

*next spread* —▷

## 1957

This track-tracing sheet is possibly the nearest we have to an official record of unidentified aerial phenomena in the sky above the British Isles. During the Cold War, RAF radars scanned the North Atlantic and North Sea for Soviet intruders 24 hours every day of the year. Radar operators routinely made manual records of unknowns tracked on radar by marking their movements, in pencil, on tracing paper. These UFOS were designated as 'X-raids' and, if they could not be identified as friendly aircraft, RAF fighters were scrambled to intercept them. This tracing sheet was produced by Flt Lt J.S. Hassall to record the movements of strange aerial phenomena tracked by radars at RAF Ventor, Isle of Wight, on the afternoon of 29 July 1957. In his report to the Air Ministry's UFO branch, DDI (Tech), Hassall said his Type 80 radar first plotted 'X-raid 422' moving at speeds between 1000–1400 knots at a height of 42,000 feet above the English Channel. Minutes later Hassall tracked another similar echo, moving at a similar speed, then a third and a fourth. By then he had begun to doubt the tracks were genuine. His report concludes: 'It was finally decided these were spurious responses, but as they had been designated X-raids, recordings and reports were made'. AIR 20/9994

## SECURITY CLASSIFICATION

**SECRET**

DATE 29ᵗʰ July 1957 TIME 15·14 Z

R.R.U. Nº 23 S.U.   R.A.F. Ventnor.

STATION PIN POINT   Mᴋ. Pꜰ. 4836

FILE REF   VEN/S.1/9/AIR (OPS.)

RADAR HEAD   Tʏᴘᴇ 80.

..        ..

EXERCISE   Routine.

RECORDER

FG. Oꜰꜰ. Hassall.

## DISPLAY CONTROLL

### REMARKS

Tʜᴇ Fᴏʟʟᴏᴡɪɴɢ Is A Sᴋᴇᴛ

As Cʟᴏsᴇʟʏ As Pᴏssɪʙʟ

Oꜰ Tʜᴇ Rᴇsᴘᴏɴsᴇ:

X 422 Aᴛ Pɪᴄᴋᴜᴘ:

Gʀᴏᴜɴᴅ Sᴘᴇ

Rᴀɴɢᴇs Aɴᴅ Bᴇᴀʀɪɴɢ

Iɴɪᴛɪᴀʟ Pɪᴄᴋᴜᴘ  =   18

Fᴀᴅᴇ        =

<u>STATION REPORTING</u>
<u>CONTROLLERS REMARKS</u>

It Was Finally Decided That These Were
Spurious Responses, But As They Had
Been Designated X-Raids, Recordings
And Reports Were Made For Information

<u>LEGEND</u>

O .INITIAL PLOT
↓ DIRECTIONAL ARROW
(1203) TIME AT 5 MIN INTERVALS
MIN INTERVALS MKD ONLY
H, X, F. etc. IDENTIFICATION
2/48 STRENGTH & HEIGHT
S or F SPEED
E ESTIMATED HEIGHT
<u>NOTE</u> FULL ANCILLARY
INITIALLY & ON CHANGE
⌒ FADED
RD REMOVED
R REAPPEARED
R.I. RE-IDENTIFIED

BG   CG   DG   EG   FG

1516 z

⊙ S 422/1/NH

BF   CF   DF   EF   FF

R. X 422/1/42

R. X 422/1/NH/F

One of the most mysterious images in the MoD files is a colour photograph of a little girl, holding a bunch of flowers, as a strange space-suited figure looms behind her head. The photograph was taken by a Carlisle fireman, Jim Templeton, of his five-year-old daughter Elizabeth on a family day out in May 1964. Jim and his family saw nothing unusual at the time, as they enjoyed the wild scenery of Burgh Marsh, in northern Cumbria. But when he collected the processed film the shop assistant said: 'That's a marvellous photograph, but it's rather spoilt by the big man behind her!' When Jim took a closer look he was amazed to find that on one of the prints, standing just behind his daughter's head, was a large figure dressed like an astronaut in a white suit with a dark visor. Jim sent the negatives for scrutiny to Kodak and the Cumbrian police. Both said the image had not been tampered with. After the story was featured in the *Cumberland News* Jim's photograph was re-published in newspapers as far away as Australia. Hundreds of letters arrived from across the world at the Templeton household, many offering esoteric explanations for the 'Solway Spaceman'. Jim was also visited by two mysterious men dressed in black suits and bowler hats, who drove a brand new black Jaguar car and asked to see where the photograph was taken. They referred to each other by numbers and said they were from 'the Ministry'. But the surviving RAF and MoD files that mention the 'Solway Spaceman' do not provide any clues to the identity of the strange figure in the photograph. Over the years the case became a *cause celebre* in UFOlogy and the image has been featured in many TV programmes, books and articles. Jim died in 2011 at the age of 91 with the mystery unsolved. His last words on the subject were: 'It is up to you to draw your own conclusions. I am sure someone out there knows what it was and where it was from'. AIR 2/17526, DEFE 24/1983/1

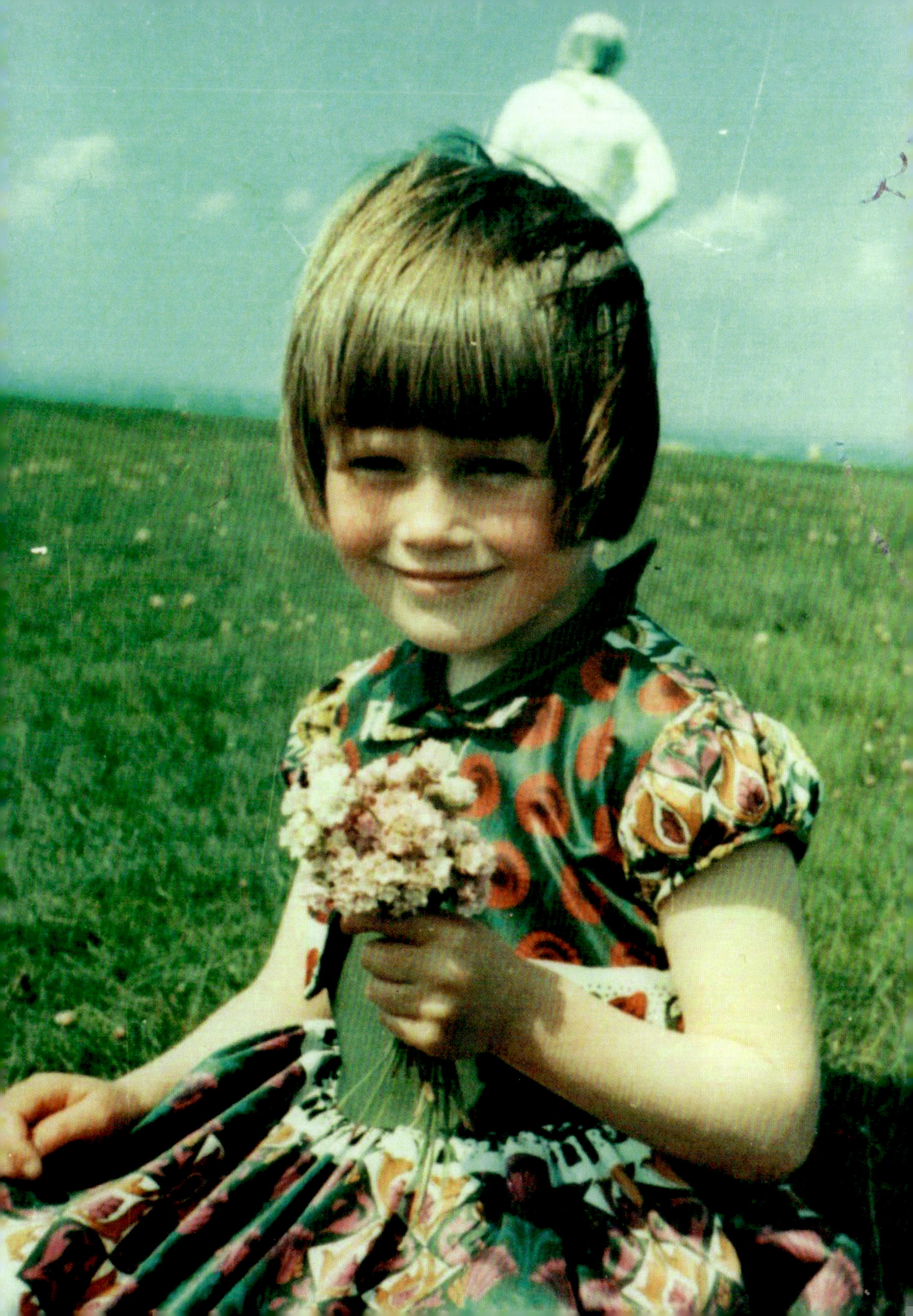

Police officers are generally considered to be some of the best UFO witnesses as they are trained to observe accurately as part of their duties. In the early hours of a cold, clear morning in January 1966, PC Colin Perks, 28, was on foot patrol in the backstreets of Wilmslow, Cheshire, when he heard 'a high pitched whine'. Turning around, he was startled by a greenish-grey glow in the sky just a few hundred yards away. 'I stopped in my tracks and was unable to believe what I could see,' he wrote in his report to the Chief Constable. 'The object was the length of a bus (30 feet) ... and 20 feet wide. It was elliptical in shape and emanated a greenish grey glow which I can only describe as an eerie greeny colour'. PC Perks said he appeared to be looking at the flat underside of the object. The sketch he drew of the UFO, 20 minutes after his experience, resembles an upturned jelly-mould. It remained motionless for five seconds before moving off sideways at fast speed to the east. Three weeks later he was interviewed by an RAF intelligence officer. His report said 'there is no reason to doubt the fact that this constable saw something completely foreign to his previous experience'. AIR 2/17983

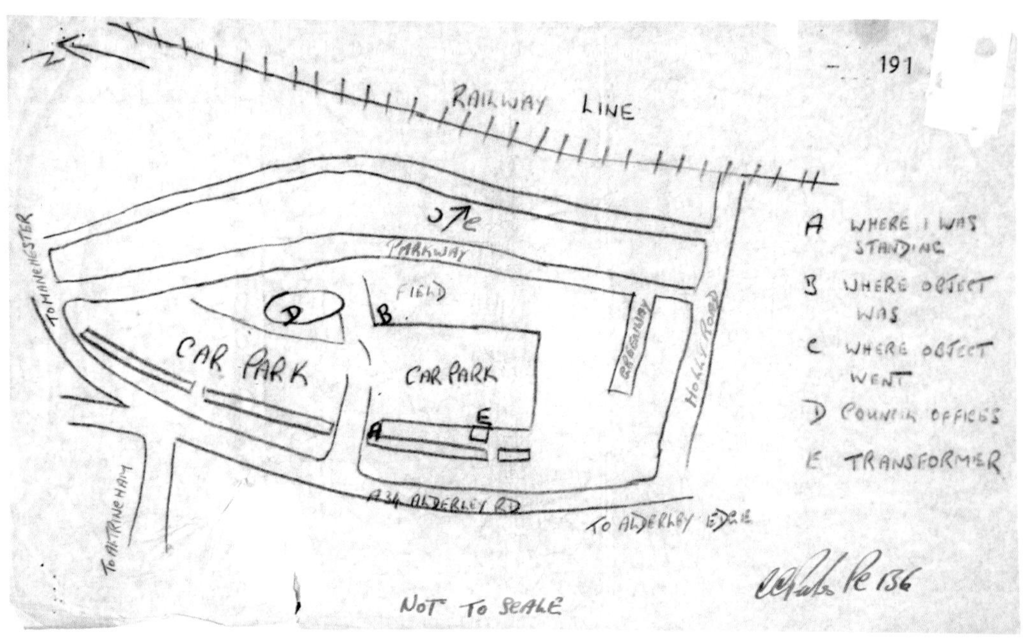

RAILWAY LINE
TO MANCHESTER
PARKWAY
SITE
FIELD
D
B
CAR PARK
CAR PARK
GASGANTRY
HOLLY ROAD
A
E
TO MOTRINGHAM
A34 ALDERLEY RD
TO ALDERLEY EDGE
A WHERE I WAS STANDING
B WHERE OBJECT WAS
C WHERE OBJECT WENT
D COUNCIL OFFICES
E TRANSFORMER
NOT TO SCALE
PC 136


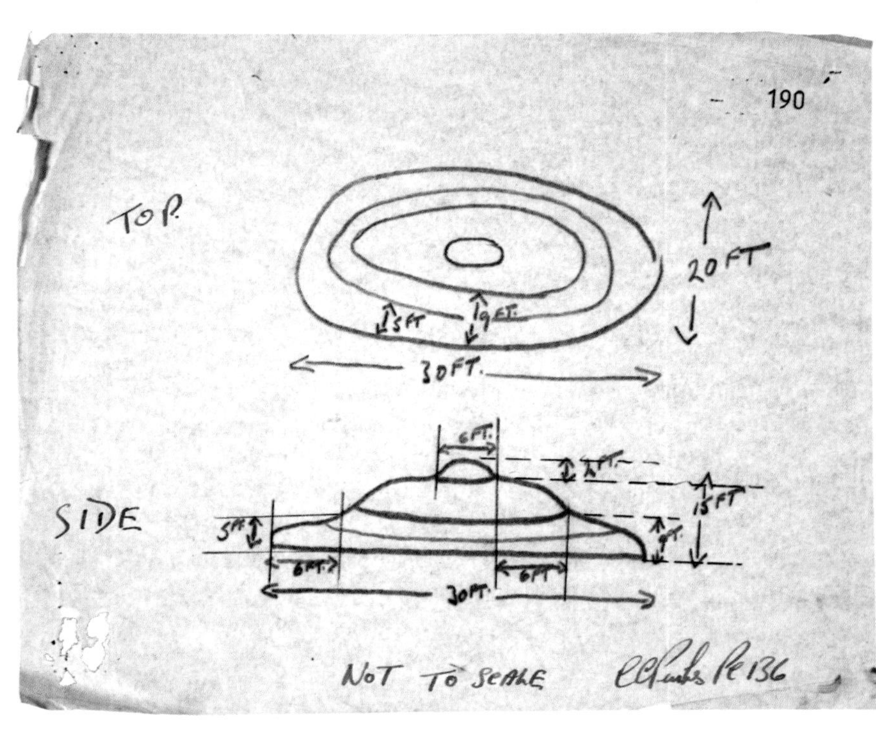

— 190
TOP.
20 FT
5 FT
19 FT.
30 FT.
SIDE
6 FT.
3 FT.
15 FT
5 FT
6 FT.
6 FT.
30 FT.
NOT TO SCALE
PC 136

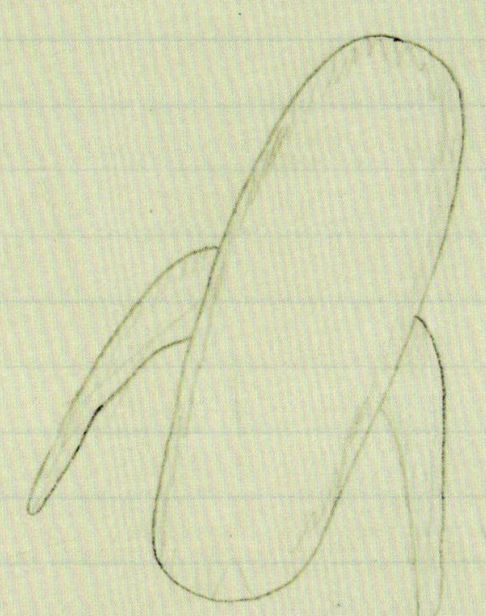

THE OBJECT LOOKED LIKE THIS THROUGH BINOCULARS.
(It was tilted up at an angle similar to the drawing).
NOTES:- distinct edge, no portholes or windows, no lights.
No vapour trail, no noise, no exhaust trail.
No visible attachment to the ground whatsoever.

1966

Teenager Nicholas Langford was so struck by the object he saw early one morning in the sky above Wolverhampton in March 1966 that he sent an account, with a drawing, to the Ministry of Defence. Nicholas, 15, was sitting in a car with his father waiting for a friend before a trip to Wales when he spotted a 'bright, yellowish-white glowing light' hanging in the eastern sky behind some trees. 'At first I thought it was a streetlamp,' he explained. 'But after a while... the object had moved from its original position... about thirty degrees above the horizon'. Nicholas asked his father for binoculars and, through them, saw it was oval in shape and had swept-back wings like a Hawker Hunter jet fighter. But this object was completely silent. 'The strange thing about it is that it was gently pulsating – I noticed this very clearly', he recalled. 'My father and friend saw it also through the binoculars and it wasn't imagination'. After 30 minutes, with the object still in the sky, the trio carried on with their journey. Nicholas continued to watch the object as it moved, 'very, very slowly... I did not notice when it disappeared'. AIR 2/17984

*next spread* —▷

1967

One of the few accounts in the MoD archives that resulted in a field investigation was the strange story of Angus Brooks. He was a retired civil aviation official who had worked on the Comet jet airliner and was familiar with many types of aircraft. On the afternoon of 26 October 1967 Brooks said he was out walking his two dogs during a fierce gale on the deserted Moigne Downs in southern Dorset when he decided to shelter by lying flat on his back in a hollow. In his letter to the MoD he said: 'Almost immediately I observed a fine contrail [that] could have been a reflection of a "craft" very high in the sky over the Portland area. This disappeared and into my view, descending at lightning speed came the "craft" which decelerated with what appeared to be immensely powerful reverse thrust to level out at approximately a quarter of a mile to the south of my position at 2–300 foot height'. He precisely described the UFO as 150 feet in length, with a central circular chamber from the front of which extended

41

a long 'fuselage'. Three more long fuselages extended from the rear and these moved to positions equidistant around the centre of the craft, so that it took the shape of a cross. Brooks said he lay still for 20 minutes, fearing that he might be 'captured' if he moved. He noticed that the silent, insect-like object appeared to be constructed from some translucent material as '[it] took on the colour of the sky above it and changed with clouds passing over it'. Then, the two central fuselages folded back to their original position and the UFO disappeared in the direction of the Winfrith Atomic Research Station. During the sighting his pet Alsatian returned to his side and appeared upset. He believed that she might have been distressed by a VHF sound emitted by the UFO although he had heard nothing himself during the experience. After he reported the experience to the police a three-man team arrived at his home from the MoD's UFO desk to question him and visit the location. One of the trio, a RAF psychologist called Alex Cassie, came to believe that Brooks experienced a vivid daydream when he lay down to shelter from the wind. He suggested the dream had been influenced by reports of a cross-shaped UFO – that received mass media coverage in the UK shortly before his experience. Cassie's report to the MoD said 'his [Brooks] instant knowledge and certainty of the size and distance and its intent, are all suggestive of the immediate and inexplicable awareness which are characteristic of many dreams'. Although he could not prove his theory was the correct one Cassie said 'it just seems possible, even likely'. But he could not resist adding that 'if his experience can't be explained in some such way, then maybe he saw an extra-terrestrial object!' However, in the formal letter sent to Brooks, UFO desk officer Leslie Ackhurst said the team did not doubt that he had an experience 'for which no proven explanation can be given' but added: 'we have concluded that you did not see a "craft" either man-made or from outer space'. It added: 'While it would be intellectually arrogant to dispute the hypothesis that in the infinity of space there could be other intelligent life... we have no proof of this [and] our radar cover is such that we are also quite satisfied that there is no clandestine aerial activity over the United Kingdom under terrestrial control. Your report does not give us cause to alter or amend these conclusions.' AIR 20/11890

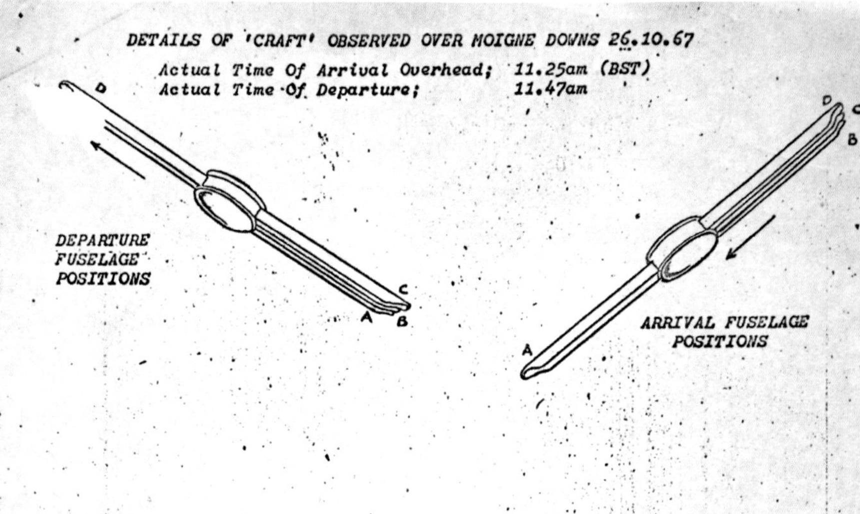


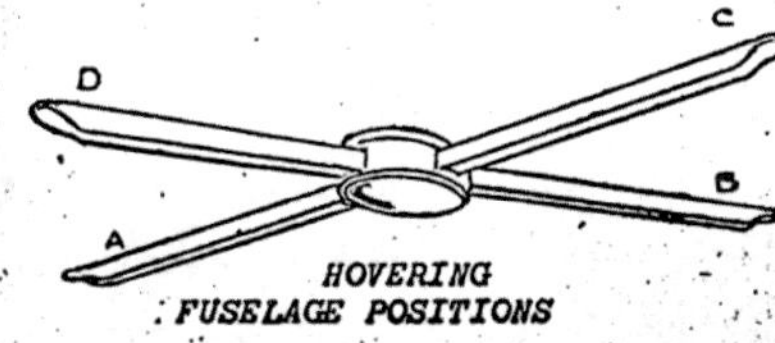


Dimensions( Approx ):
Centre Chamber: Diameter 25ft.
               Height 12ft

Fuselages: Length 75ft Hgt. 7ft Width 8ft.

DETAILS OF RIBBING OR FINS
ON UNDERSIDE OF FUSELAGES

Position of observation:
Grid Ref. 755833 on Ordnance Survey Map (1" to 1 mile) Gt. Britain Sheet 178
                                                              (DORCHESTER).

Observer:  Angus Brooks,
           (ex BOAC Comet Flight, Flight Admin.
                                   Officer.

Between 8.30 and 8.50 on the evening of Friday, 25 April, the MoD switchboard in London was jammed by phone calls from people across the British Isles reporting a fireball-shaped UFO moving north to south. They described the object as 'cigar shaped, orange/yellow in colour with a greenish glow and a long tail... very bright and apparently dropping fragments' to earth. RAF Fighter Command received 30 separate reports including two from pilots of civilian aircraft, one of whom reported a near miss with the object 'which crossed his nose from left to right heading northwest about 2,000 yards ahead'. Although some said it was low, others said it appeared to disappear above cloud and some callers reported seeing 'a mysterious flaming object' crash into a hillside in North Wales. Two detailed accounts were sent to MoD complete with sketches of the object, seen from Stourport-on-Severn, Worcestershire. One type-written account, sent by Mr D.G. Bratt, said his attention had been attracted by 'a pale jade green flash, then a bright white object with short stubby tail appearing like two cones joined at their bases in [an] envelope of white gaseous matter as shown on attached sketch'. He said this object moved in a straight line, gained height and had 'similar dimension to a large air liner'. He was 'firmly convinced this was a UFO or flying saucer'. Soon afterwards astronomers from the Royal Observatory in Belfast identified the UFO as a meteorite. Fragments from the object were reported falling on Northern Ireland. One piece made a hole in the roof of a police building in Lisburn – triggering fears of a terrorist bomb attack – whilst another left a small crater in a field. Mr Bratt remained unconvinced. In a follow-up letter to MoD he said: 'In my opinion the [meteorite] theory is incorrect as the object which I saw does not match up to any descriptions of meteorites or comets in books on astronomy'. AIR 20/12058

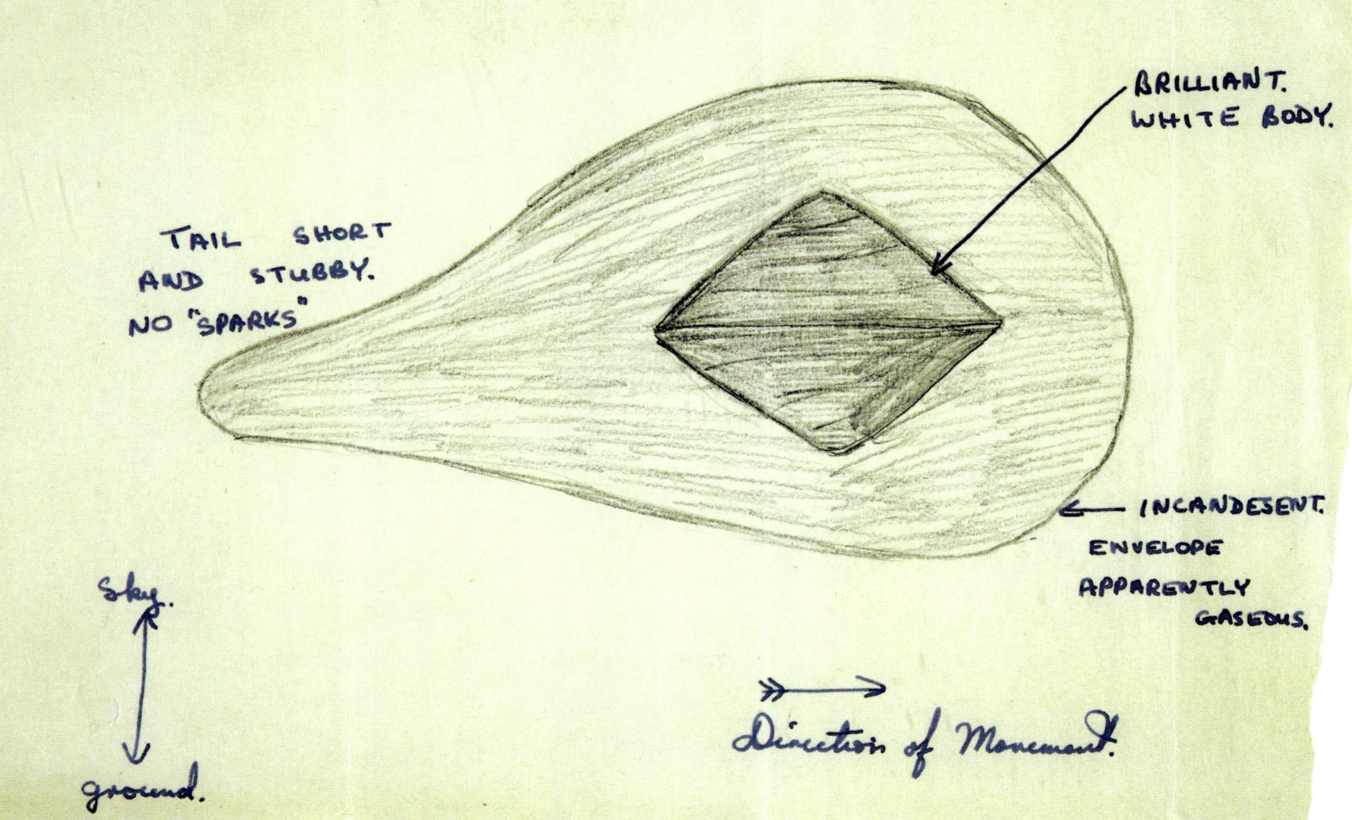
BRILLIANT.
WHITE BODY.
TAIL SHORT
AND STUBBY.
NO "SPARKS"
INCANDESENT.
ENVELOPE
APPARENTLY
GASEOUS.
Sky.
ground.
Direction of Movement.
37

SEEN FRIDAY 25TH APRIL
9.15 P.M.

COLOURS FANTASTICALLY VIVID.

ANGLE OF FLIGHT.

DEFINITELY CLIMB
TRAVELLING VERY
WOULD SEEM TO
THEORY OF FAL

NO SOUND.

BRIGHT GLOWING
LIGHT.

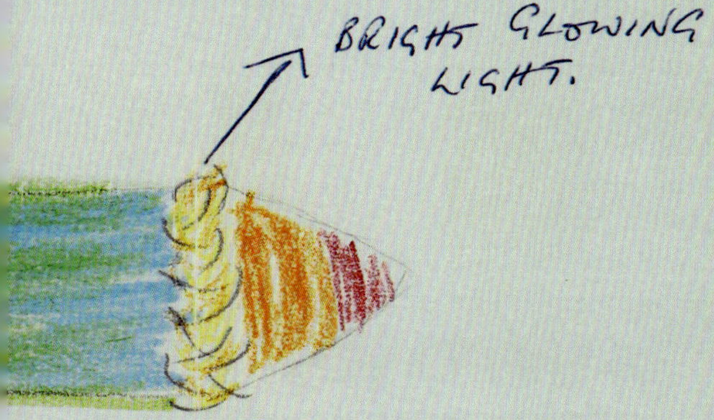

OUT OF
SIGHT
BEHIND TREES

-INDICATE
...EORITE.

In the early hours of an August morning Mary Weare detected a silent, unlighted cigar-shaped UFO hovering above fields near her home in Chalfont St Peter, near Amersham in Buckinghamshire. Mrs Weare had seen UFOS on several occasions before. But this object was different because it projected a beam of light downwards onto a low-lying cloud. 'It was quite clear and distinct although the beam itself had a nebulous quality,' she told BBC Radio Oxford. 'I could see a series of symbols, or signs, thrown into relief by the beam and I had time to copy them onto paper with a pencil in the light thrown from the craft... as I was copying them down every tree, every chimney pot, every rooftop was as light as day itself and the birds began to sing'. Suddenly the beam was switched off and the UFO moved off at a terrific speed, creating a tremendous vibration that shook her bedroom. 'Dogs in the neighbourhood were all barking and my two dogs were faintly whimpering as they do when there is a thunderstorm,' she added. Mrs Weare reported her experience to Amersham police and sent a copy of her pencil-drawing to the MoD. In his response UFO desk head Anthony Davies said the 'hieroglyphs' drawn by Mrs Weare were similar to astrological symbols in common use and 'perhaps she was allowing subconsciously her inner astrological interest to suggest images to her inner vision'. AIR 20/12399

YOUR REF:
OUR REF:
DATE
1st line
2nd LINE
FINAL FIGURE


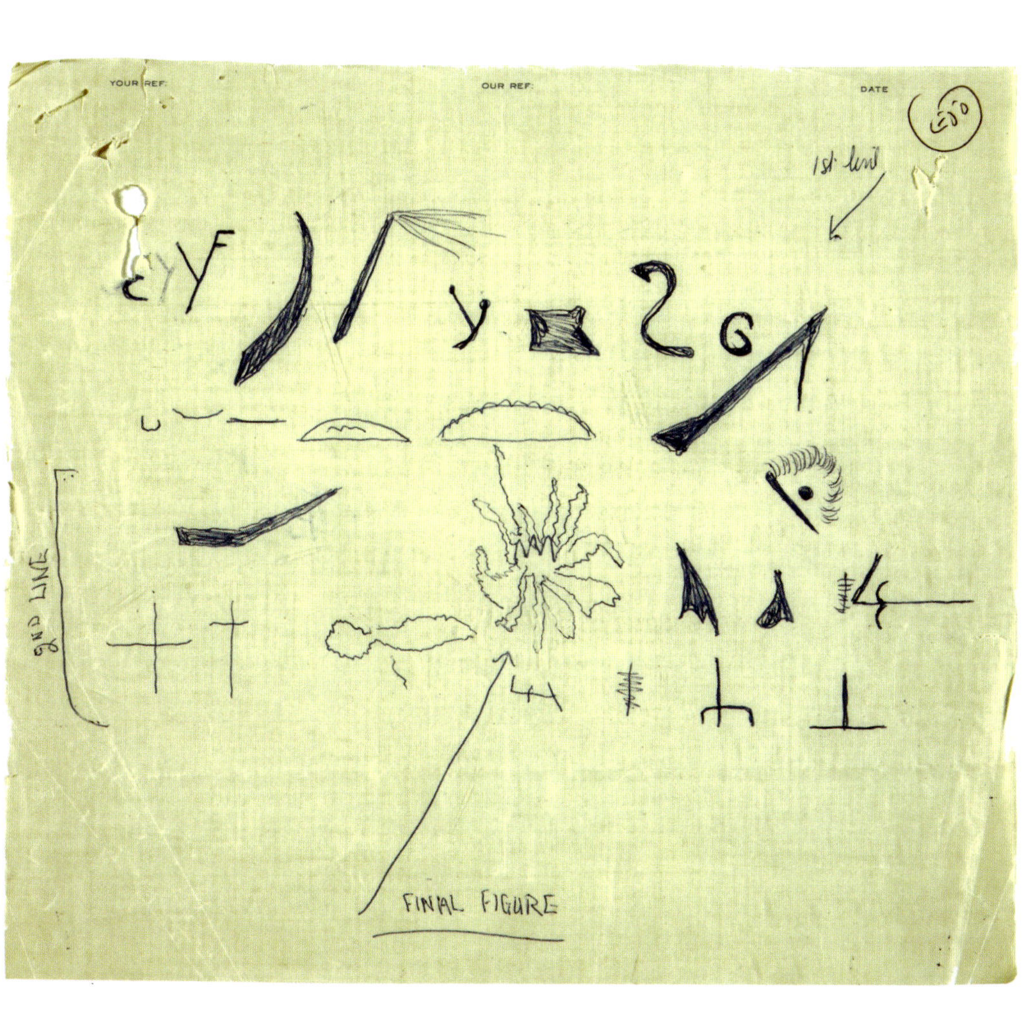

SIGHTED FOR 5 minutes approx on SAT. 25 MARCH

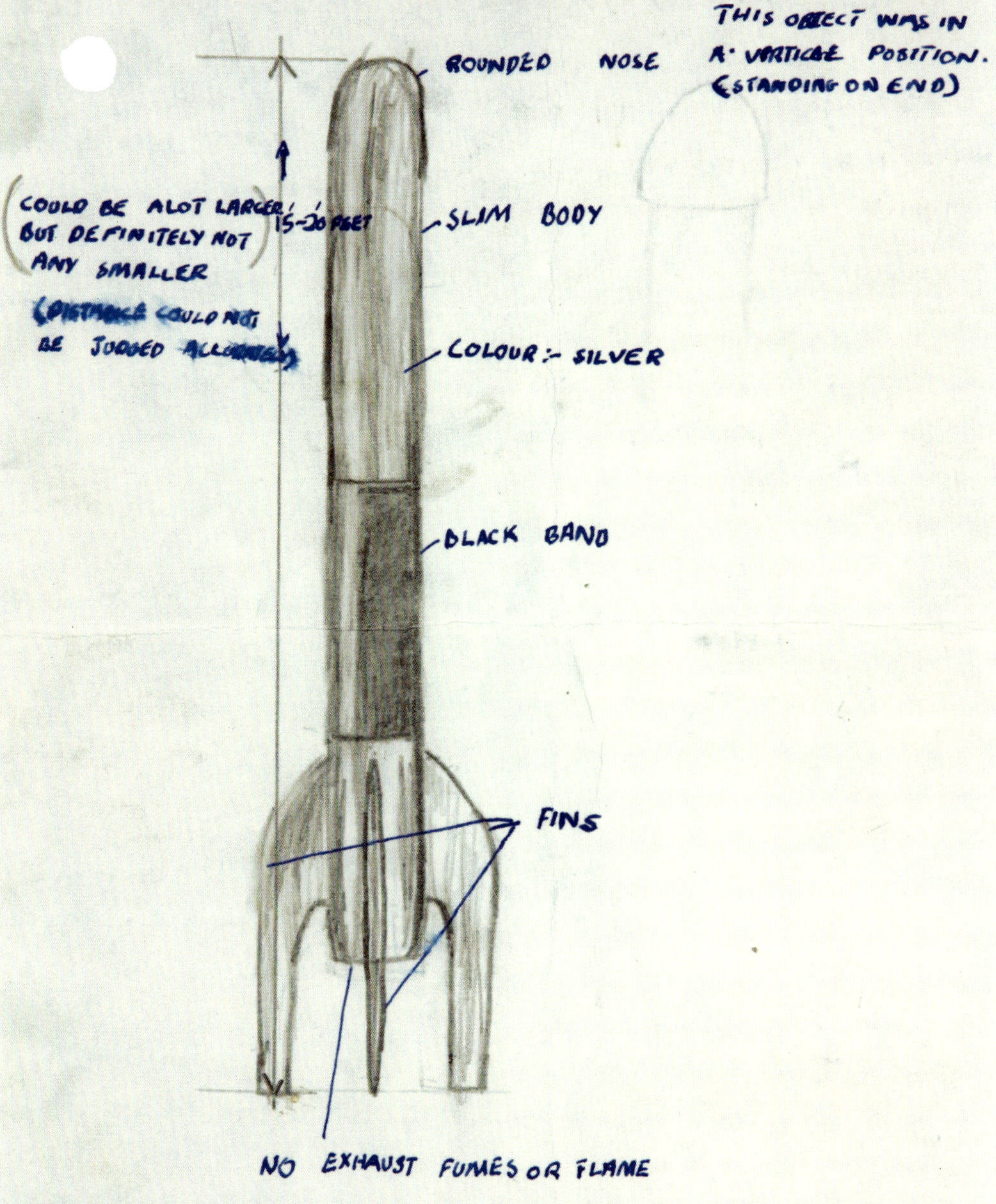

THIS OBJECT WAS IN A VERTICAL POSITION. (STANDING ON END)

ROUNDED NOSE

SLIM BODY

COLOUR :- SILVER

BLACK BAND

( COULD BE ALOT LARGER, BUT DEFINITELY NOT ANY SMALLER

15-20 FEET

(DISTANCE COULD NOT BE JUDGED ALTOGETHER)

FINS

NO EXHAUST FUMES OR FLAME

Some artists impressions of UFOs betray the influence of popular culture. Drawings in the MoD archives resemble futuristic flying saucers, rockets and spaceships from TV shows, movies and comic books. These drawings were sent to the MoD by a woman and three teenagers from Hampstead in North London who saw a 'rocket-shaped' object with four fins and a black band around its centre in daylight one afternoon in March 1972. Her 16-year-old son watched the object through binoculars as it travelled vertically into the sky. UFO desk officer Miss G. J. Jamieson suggested they had seen a climbing VC-10 aircraft. 'The apparent vertical orientation could have resulted from some optical illusion due to the lack of fixed reference points near to the object,' she added. But the object drawn by two of the witnesses more closely resembles a WW2 V2 rocket or one of the futuristic rescue vehicles that appear in the TV science-fiction series *Thunderbirds*. The series, created by Gerry and Sylvia Anderson, premiered on the ITV network in September 1965 and was repeated frequently during the 1970s. AIR 20/12402

'Could you, possibly, give me any idea as to what it was I saw in the sky?' The wife of a RAF Wing Commander posed this question in a letter addressed to the MoD. At 6 am on Sunday, 6 October 1974, she was making tea on the first floor of their house in Northwood, Middlesex, when a light in the sky caught her attention. Initially she thought it was a star but this idea was dispelled when it moved across the sky from west to east. Then she assumed it must be a satellite but, when it changed direction, she grabbed a pair of binoculars to examine it further. As she focused she was startled to see 'what looked like alternate lighted windows' around a dark central object. 'It could not possibly have been a plane of any kind, nor a helicopter... it must have been large, it was not very high in the sky. I saw it very plainly and it was obviously metal of some kind, not a balloon or a reflection'. No one else was around so she immediately sketched the object and gave it to her husband when he returned home on leave. He showed it to a meteorological officer 'who had no idea what it may be, and he suggested that I should write to you'. AIR 2/18958

6am. Oct. 6.

The 'lighted window effect, was visible all the way round it. It appeared to be a very large object. There was no other shape through the night binoculars. There was no other shape attached to it, at all, and it was perfectly clearly visible through the glasses; was obviously metal (not balloon, or reflection) moved at the speed of a 'plane and looked like a star without the glasses.

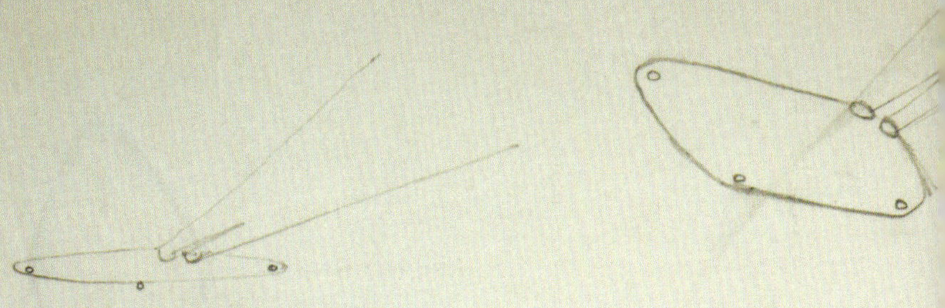

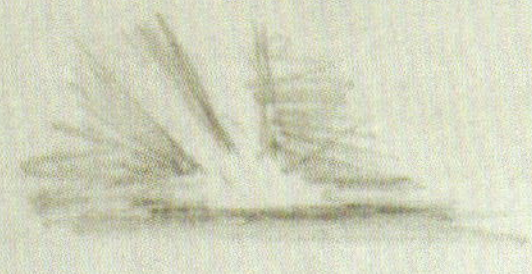

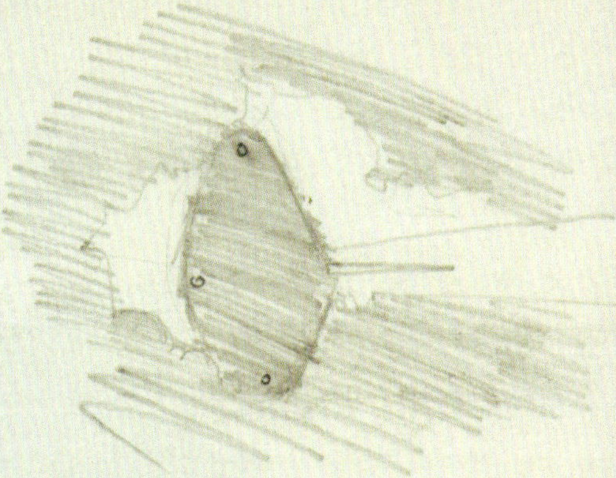

EXHIBIT 1

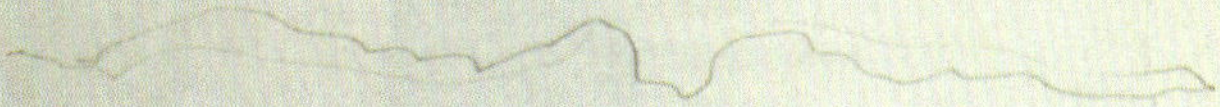

SKETCH PLAN OF
SCANTLINGS AS PER
STATEMENT

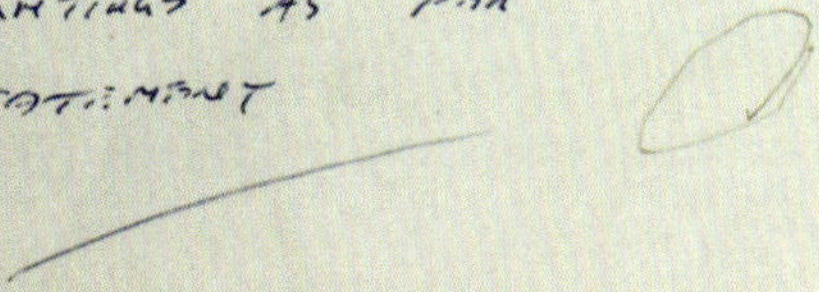

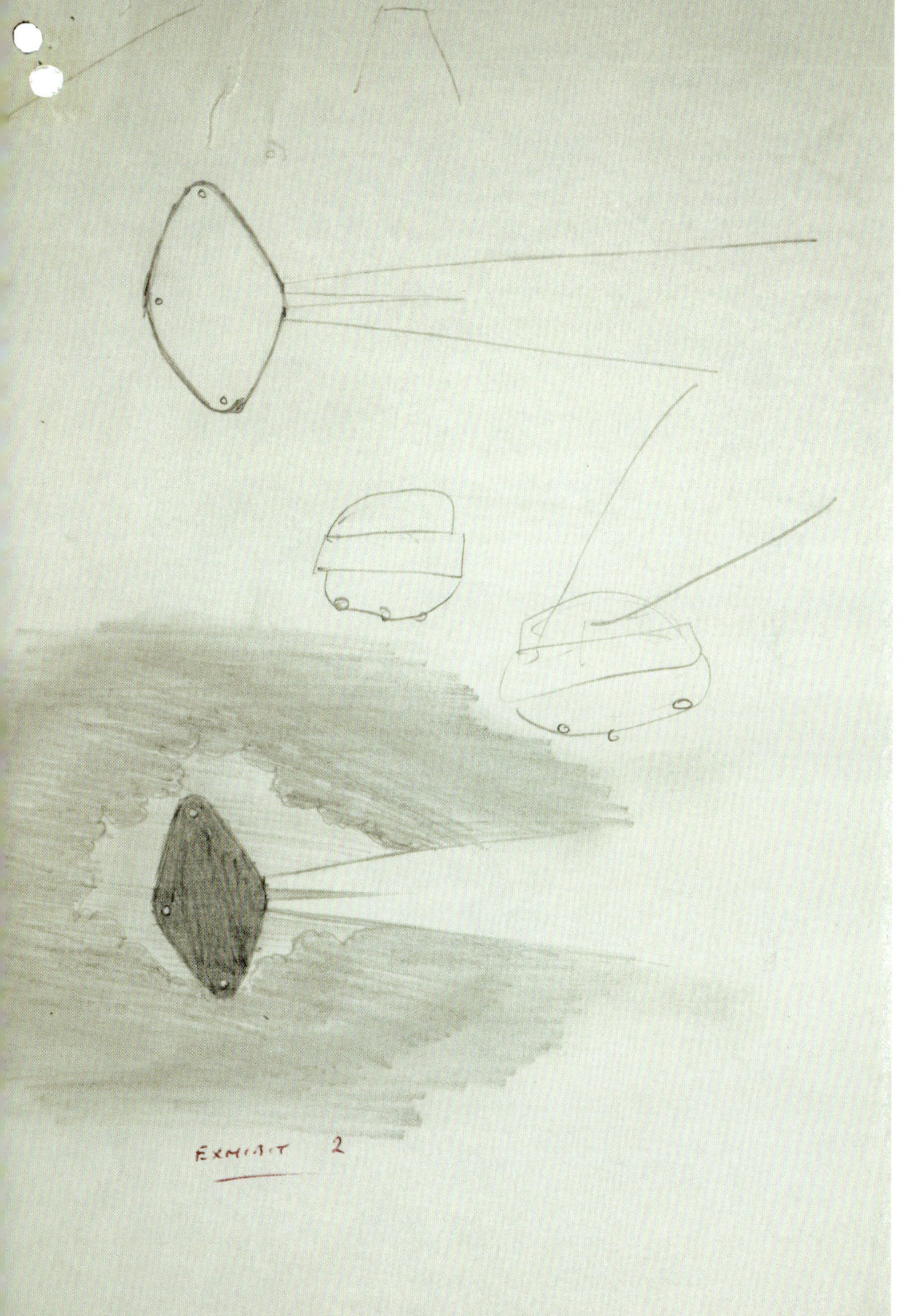

EXHIBIT 2

## 1974

A 25-year-old artist and his wife had just pulled their car onto the drive of their house in Stapleford Tawney, Essex, at 8.30 on the evening of 5 October 1974 when they noticed a strange object in the sky over Ongar. At first it was stationary 'showing very powerful lights which were shining upwards and panning the sky above... to the left and right of it'. Then it moved towards Kelvedon Hatch, the site of an MoD radar station and nuclear bunker, where it searched around again before travelling towards them at high speed. As it passed them, it slowed down and the couple could see its shape and noticed the panning lights were situated at the front of the object. Constant coloured lights were also visible on the tips of its wings and as it disappeared into the distance they heard 'a very unusual whine... not the usual jet noise or the noise of a turbo-prop aircraft'. As soon as the UFO disappeared the artist went into the house and drew what he had seen. A week later he visited Abridge police station to make a formal statement that was passed to the MoD. In it he says 'although I have seen strange things at times I have found that after looking at them for a while one finds it to be just another aircraft seen from a different angle [but] this was completely different and it is the first time I have reported a sighting of what could be a U.F.O'. AIR 2/18958

*next spread* —▷

## 1975

Soon after midnight on 18 January 1975 Mr Campbell was outside his home in Harborne, Birmingham, when he saw a bright white object in the north-west. The sky was clear with a small amount of cloud and the object, moving at high speed, appeared to drop out of view towards the horizon. Mr Campbell was so 'excited and surprised' that he produced what the MoD called 'a delightful hand-painted impression' of the experience. In his letter to the UFO desk, he explained: 'The large white disc in the top left hand corner is intended to be the moon and the smaller object above the tree is intended to be Venus. Let me add, however, that neither the moon nor Venus were visible to me at the time in question; they are strictly there to give some idea of how, in size, the object I saw appeared to me'. On this occasion the MoD was able to provide a complete explanation, turning this UFO into an IFO. Checks by defence staff identified two satellites, Zond 4 and Cosmos 460, were within 100 kms at the precise time of his sighting. In his response, Mr Campbell said he 'could hardly imagine it to have been anything but what you say is likely' and he would be honoured if the MoD kept his painting in their files. AIR 2/18961

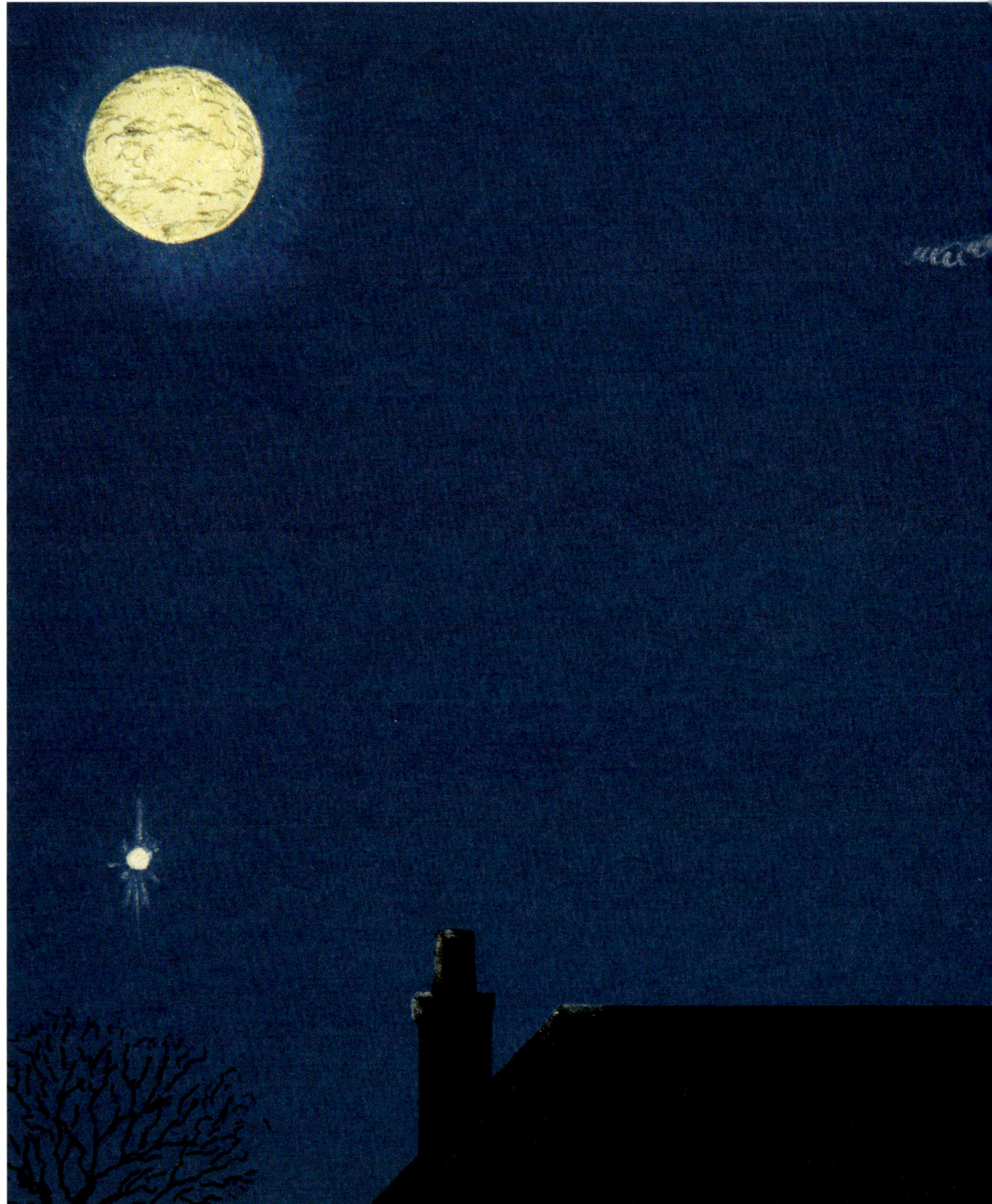

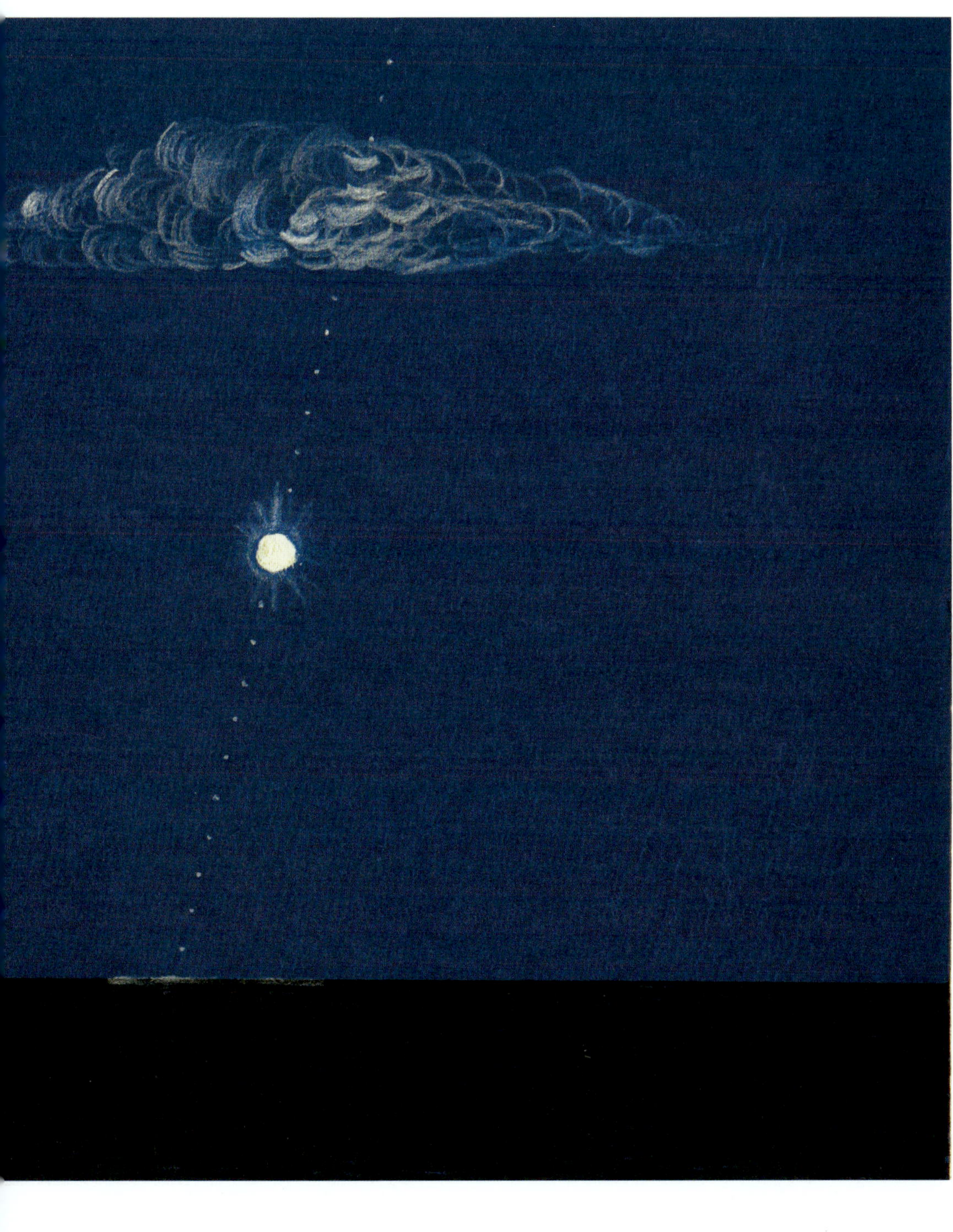

Early one dark morning in January 1976, a 13-year-old schoolboy set out from his home in Old Coulsdon, Surrey, on his paper round. It was around 6.15, the sky was clear and the stars were out. 'As I got to the end of my road I looked up and saw this object in the sky,' he explained in a handwritten letter addressed to the MoD, 'I couldn't stop looking at it'. The thing in the sky was pie shaped, quite large – larger than 'a normal aeroplane we see overhead' – and it hovered, without making a sound. 'It looked as if it was exploding [as] there was lights round the middle of the object and these were flashing... in a revolving sequence and a large beam of light was coming down on the trees from underneath the object,' he said. 'I stood watching... then ran up the hill [and] when I got to the top I looked back and it was still in the same place, it hadn't moved. I know this because of the stars'. By this point he admitted he was 'really frightened' and decided to run and not look back. Later that day his mother called the police and London airport to report his sighting but they were unable to explain what he saw. His pencil sketch of the pie-shaped UFO was placed in the Ministry of Defence files. AIR 2/18969

MUCH SMALLER
About this long ———
LOTS OF flashing lights all round
BEAM OF LIGHT
TREES

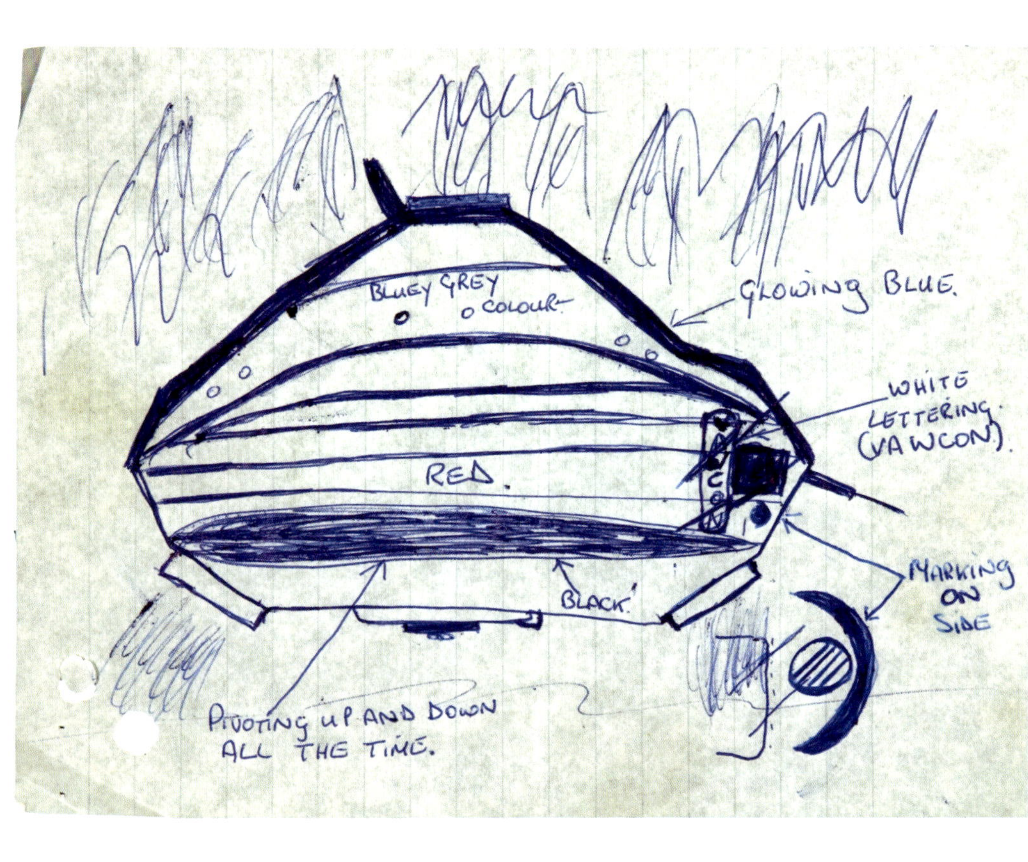

BLUEY GREY
o o COLOUR
GLOWING BLUE.
WHITE LETTERING. (VAWCON).
RED.
BLACK.
MARKING ON SIDE
PIVOTING UP AND DOWN ALL THE TIME.

The vast majority of stories from the UFO files are accounts of lights and objects seen fleetingly in the night sky. Just occasionally you come across accounts of UFOs seen at closer range. One of the oddest accounts in this category happened on 5 November 1976 and was reported to RAF Wyton in Cambridgeshire by a 29-year-old mechanical engineer. He was out walking his dog at 6 am near his parents' home at Oxmoor near Huntingdon when he saw a bizarre object descend into a field just five feet away. He said it was 'tank-like, rather square with a dome-shaped super-structure', metallic in colour with red, white and blue lights. Apart from a low-pitched hum the object was silent. The UFO did not touch down but a barrel-shaped object appeared from inside and appeared to probe the ground. At this point it turned around to face the engineer and, in his own words, he was so petrified he 'nearly had kittens'. At this point the probe was retracted and the UFO disappeared at speed, causing his dog to bolt in fear. Later that day, he produced a pen sketch of the object for an RAF investigator and revealed that he could see the letters 'VAWCON' embossed on the side of the object. He added this was the second time he had spotted the object near the playing fields. The MoD file notes that 'he reads a lot, especially books on aviation' and struck the investigator as 'imaginative'. Nevertheless a comment written on the file reads: 'Definitely a UFO'. AIR 2/18977

The release of the science fiction film *Star Wars* in 1977 coincided with a wave of UFO sightings across the UK. So many reports were made in West Wales that tabloids began to refer to part of the Pembrokeshire coast as 'the Broad Haven Triangle', after the notorious Bermuda Triangle. One spectacular sighting was reported in February by a group of ten and eleven-year-old children at Broad Haven Primary School who told their teachers a flying saucer had landed in the playground at lunchtime. Some of the boys said they had spotted a tall man dressed in a silver spacesuit standing beside the UFO. Then one afternoon in October, ten Cheshire children, aged seven to eleven years, saw an elliptical object hovering in trees beside the playground of Upton Priory Junior School in Macclesfield, before it rose and vanished. Their teacher asked them to draw what they had seen, separating them to ensure that no copying took place. The children used pencils and coloured crayons to produce the images. Their teacher passed the drawings to PC Jones of Cheshire Police, who sent them to Air Traffic Control at Preston and the MoD. He said 'there is a remarkable similarity in these sketches with regard to the UFO and its location between two trees'. DEFE 24/1206

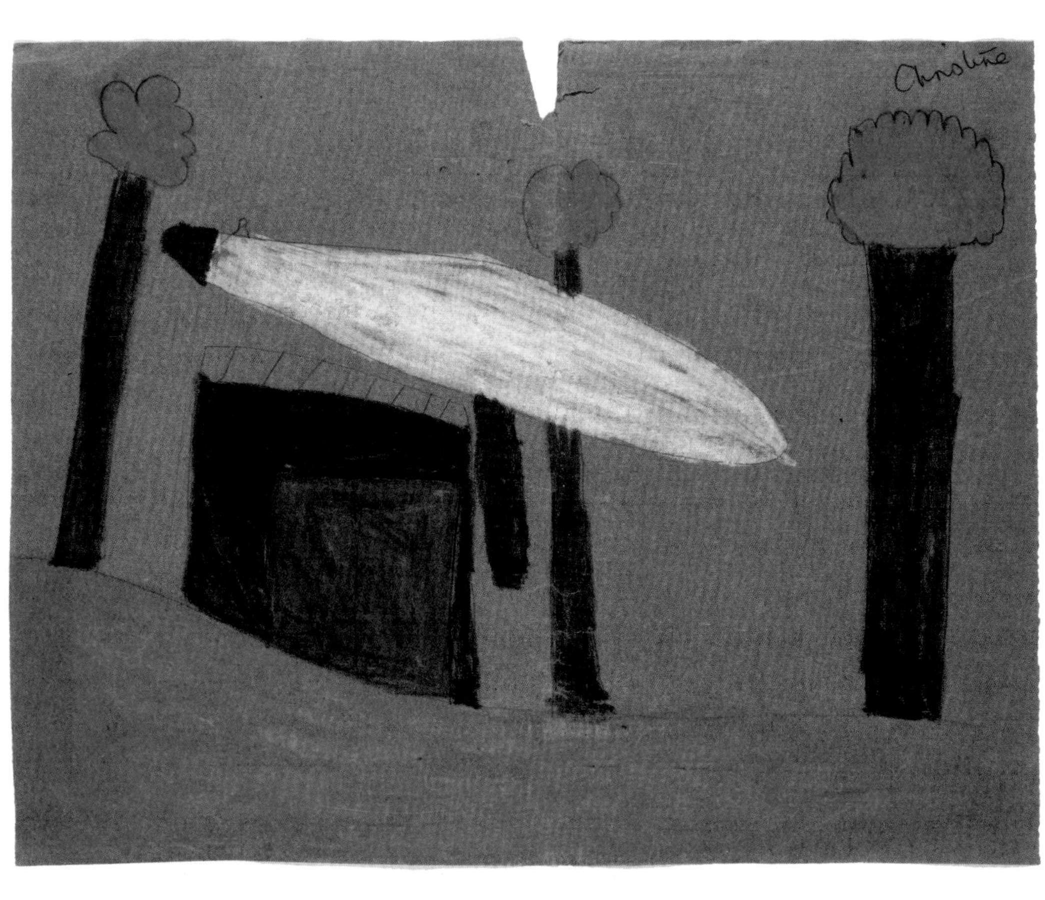

Christine

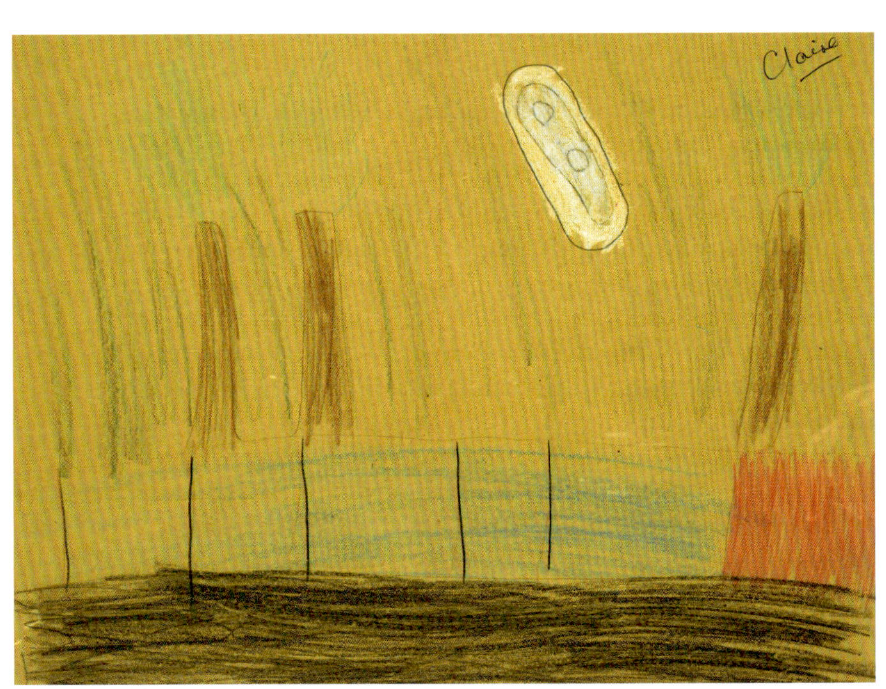
Claire

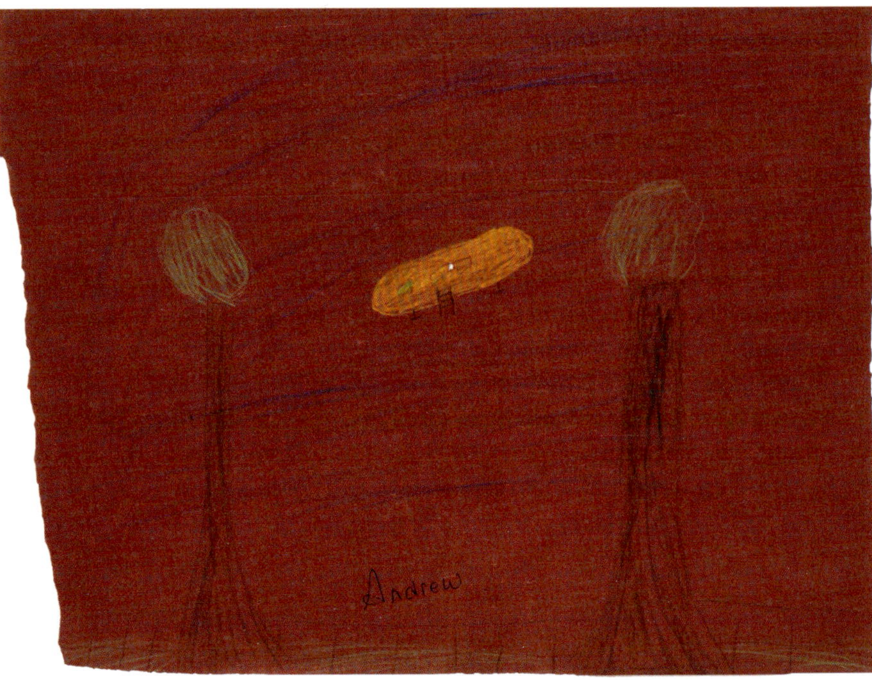
Andrew

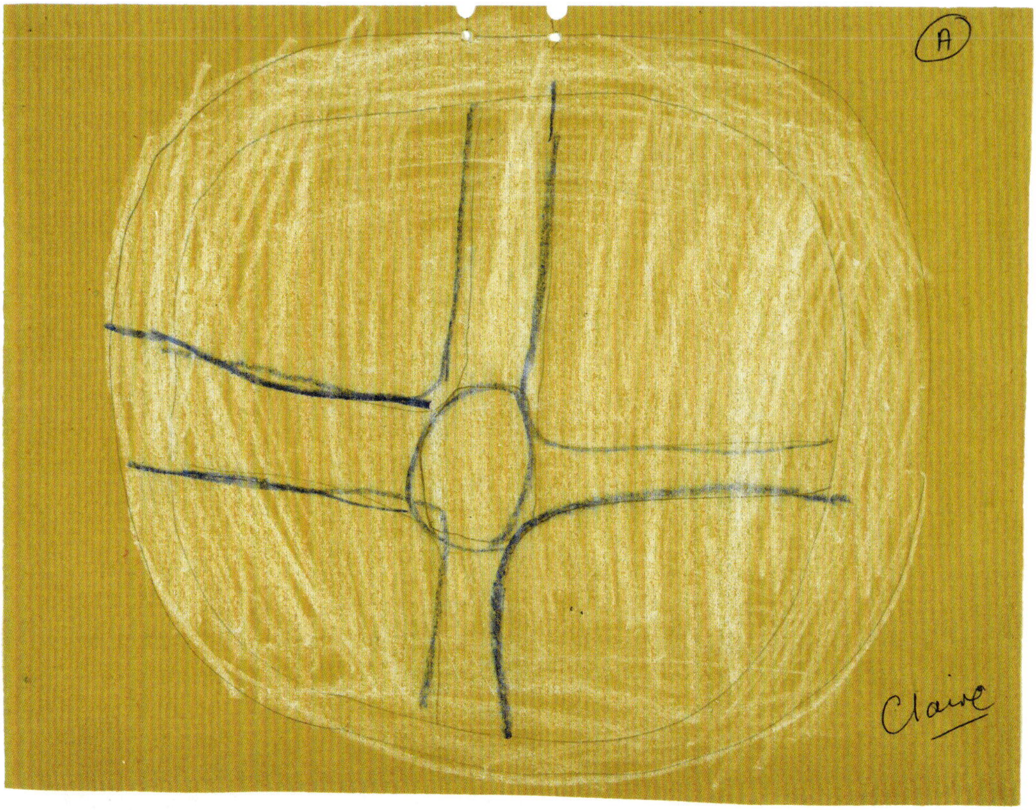

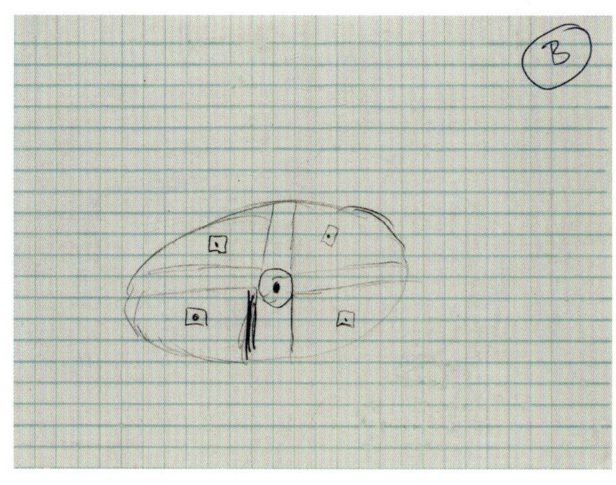

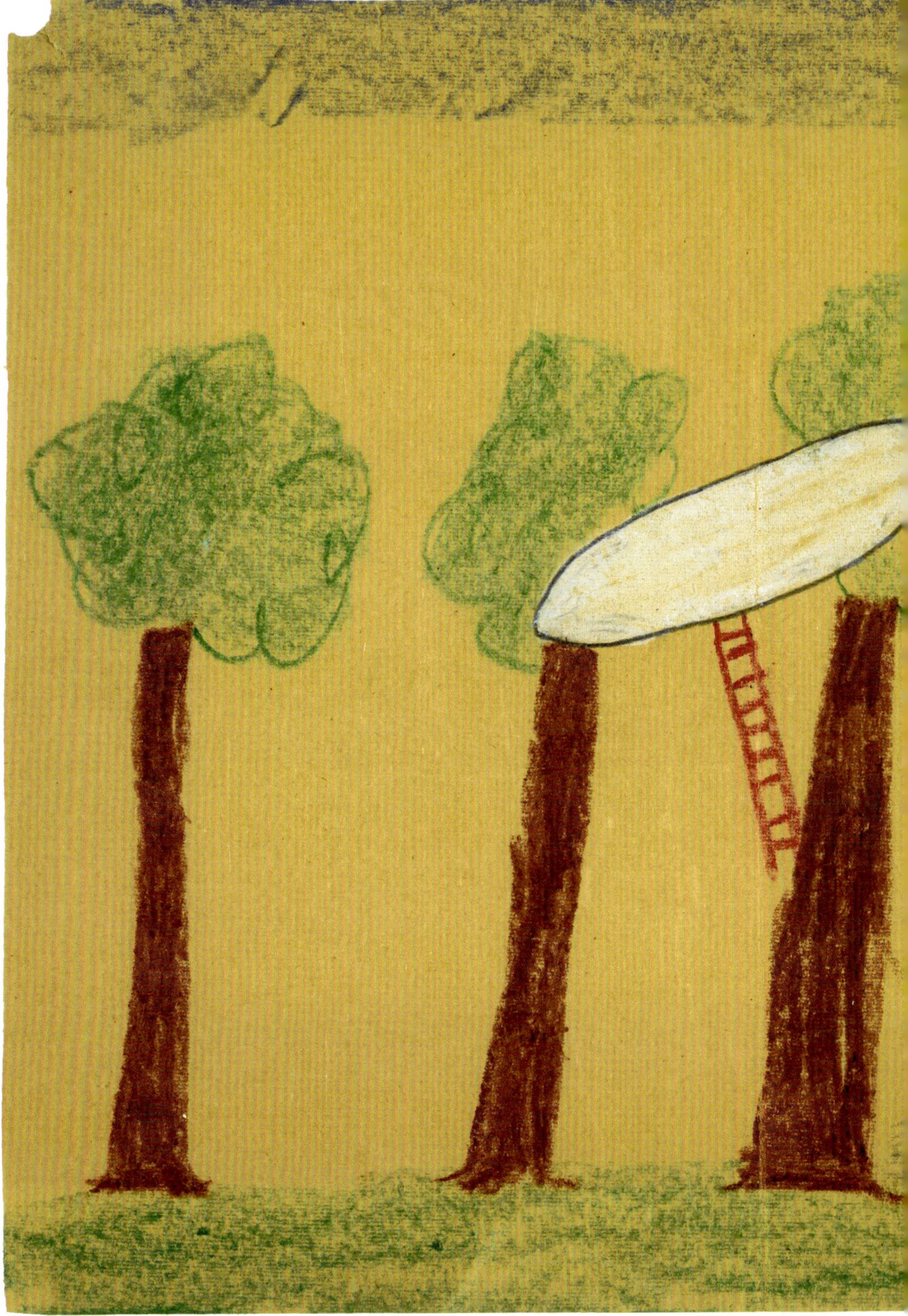

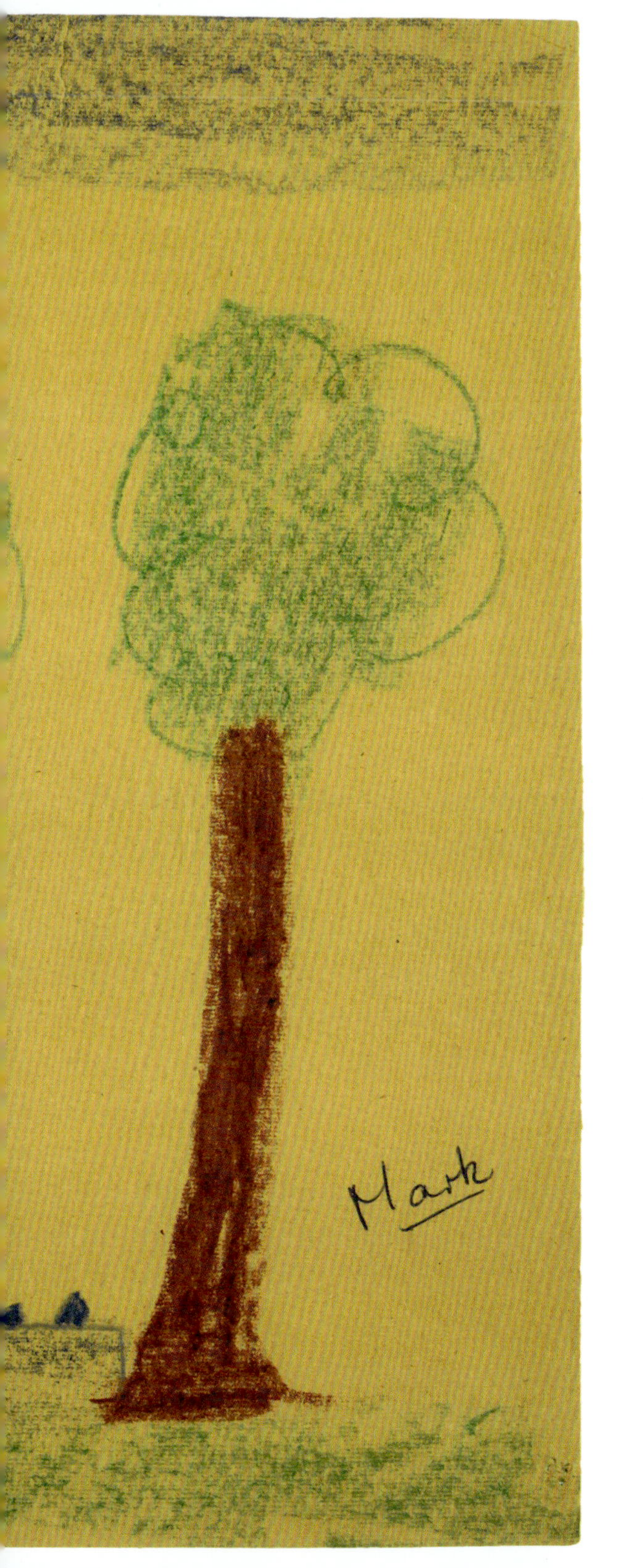
Mark

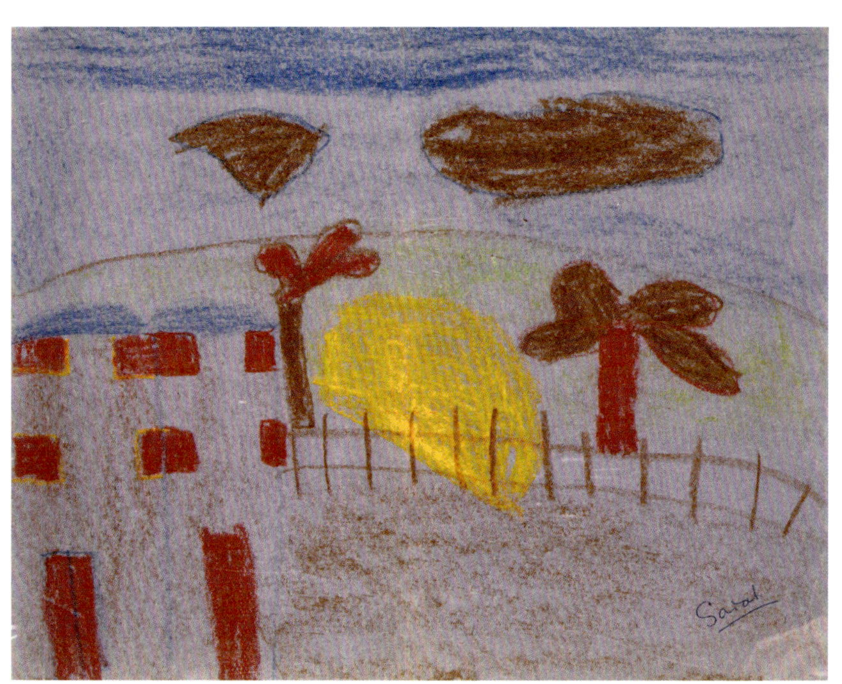

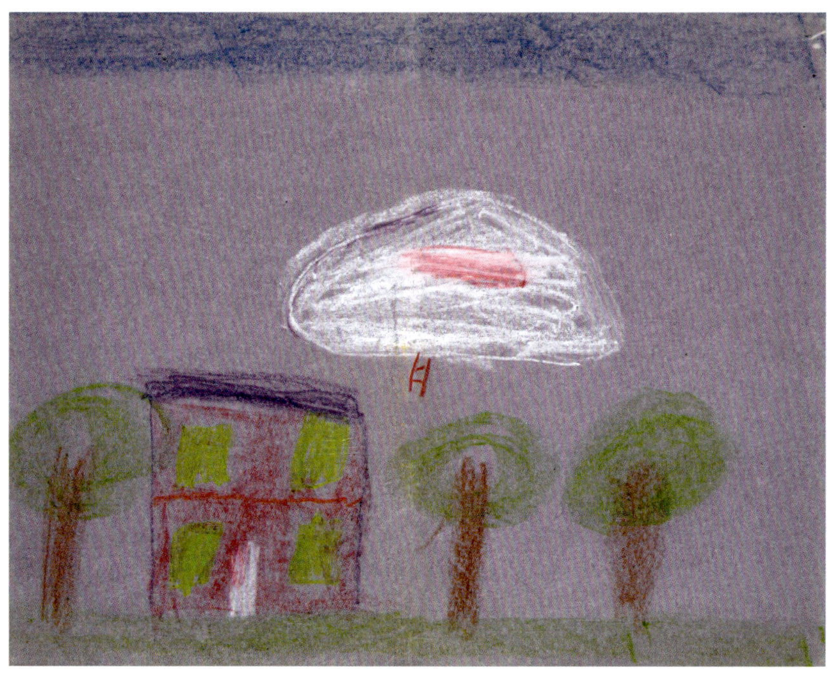

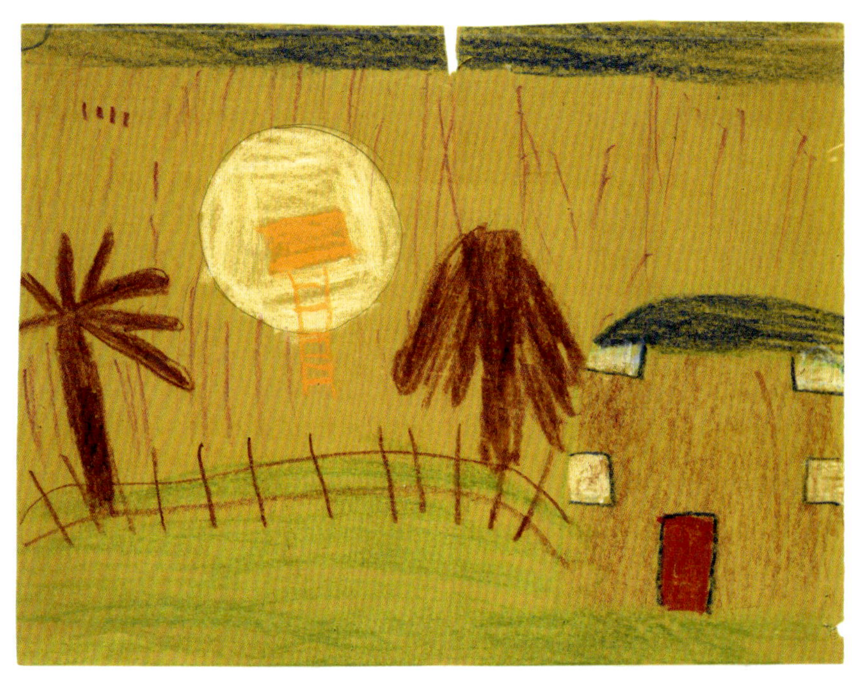

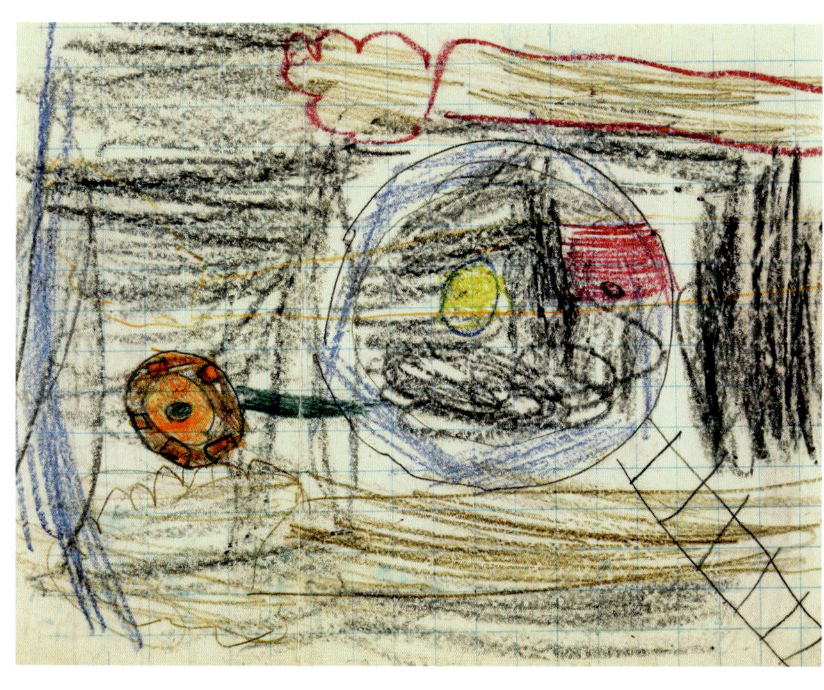

Some people see UFOs more than once and believe they are in telepathic contact with the pilots of these 'craft'. In 1977, a correspondent from Stockport in Cheshire sent a series of letters to the UFO desk telling of his sightings of flying saucers from Saturn. He enclosed a pen sketch of one UFO leaving the ringed planet en route to Earth. 'At approx. 1 am on June 26 I observed [a] UFO hovering low above and near to flats in which I live,' he explained. 'I observed the UFO from inside the flat... this object was blacked out except for a flashing spark-like white light. I intercepted the UFO using telepathy, upon doing so the [it] took immediate evasive action. I have reason to believe the object to be Soviet, although the UFO did acknowledge telepathic transmission by transmitting ring type mental picture similar to those used by UFOs identified as Drep spacecraft – indicating [a] UFO from planet Saturn'. DEFE 24/1206

Telepathic transmission by *UFO* intercepted by telepathy
similer to this but much better. Method is similer to
method used by objects identified as Drep. Picture here is
not correct as transmitted planet and rings as  transmitted
should tilt to left.              Object also not  detailed
                                        as transmitted by

                                           *UFO*

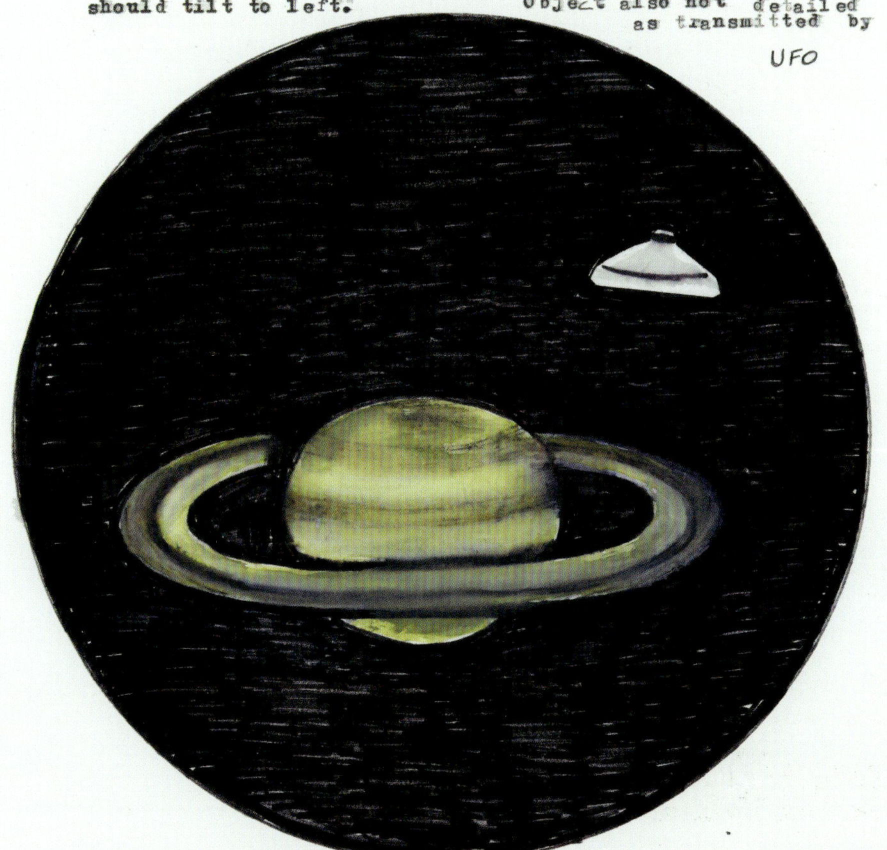

This sample of type of transmission used by *UFO*
is not any where near as good as that which was transmitted
by *UFO*. giving indication UFO planet Saturn.

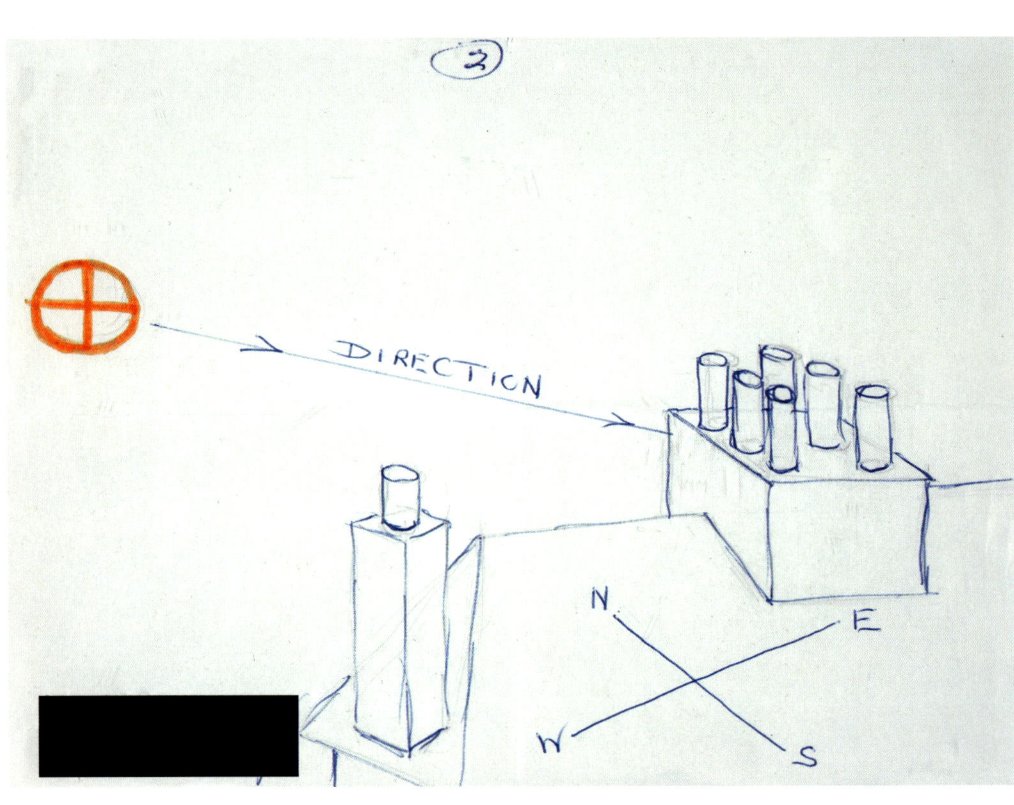

DIRECTION
N
E
W
S

A man from Eltham, in southeast London, wrote to the MoD, reporting a
UFO sighting at 9.10 am on New Year's Eve 1977. 'After washing and dressing
myself I made my way downstairs [and] when passing the landing window
I looked out to see how the weather was and looking above the house on
the other side of the road I saw an object. It was in the form of a wheel with
four spokes. The rim and spokes were an orange colour as though they were
alight and it was passing the house very slowly above the roof... I am enclos-
ing a sketch to let you know what it looked like – would you kindly forward
this to a society that deals with UFOS'. DEFE 24/1207

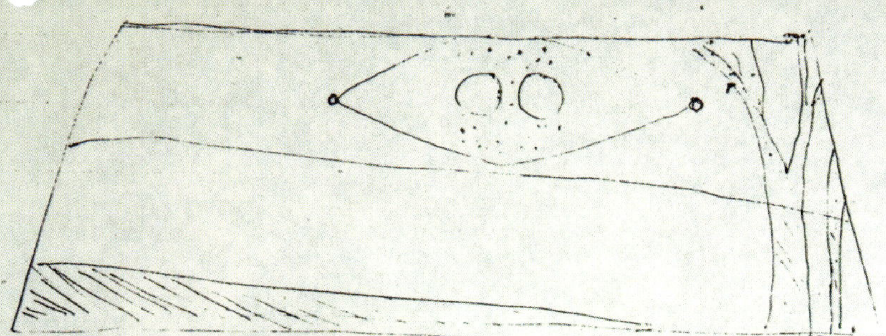

This is what the object looked like when seen through the car windscreen
when the car was stopped in a lay-by.  Object was approaching, but looked
higher in sky than in the drawing – actually about 15° above horizon.
The trunk of the tree on the other side of the road was about 10 inches
wide and about 20 feet away.  When first seen, the object was about 40°
above the horizon.

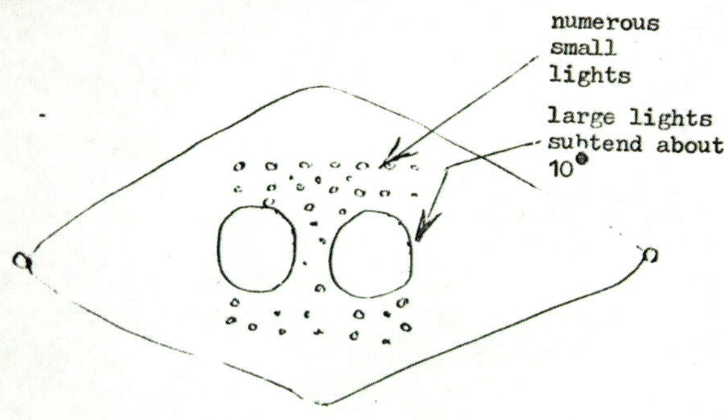

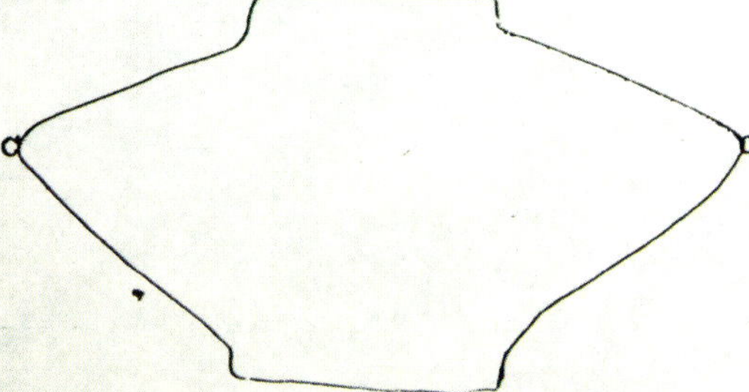

Appearance when seen directly overhead

Many of the reports received by the MoD's UFO desk were so vague and lacking in detail they were filed and forgotten. But occasionally a detailed account arrived from a credible witness that was subjected to a more detailed investigation. These drawings were made by the 27-year-old daughter of an RAF Group Captain who worked at the Aviation Medicine Training Centre. She had been a passenger in a car driven along the A12 from London towards Colchester at 9pm on 24 November 1978 when driver and passenger both saw, in the northeast, an object 'like the head-light of a car coming in to land'. It seemed to be stationary for about five to ten minutes and then came closer, as the couple stopped the car in a layby near Colchester. Stepping outside they could see a number of tiny white lights in between and around two larger central lights. She said it was 'not like any plane because there seemed to be no fuselage and wings – it was one solid shape as in my drawing'. The UFO passed directly overhead and appeared to be very large and very low. In her statement she said 'as it began to approach I was transfixed and felt overcome as though something was going to happen to us... by then I knew it was nothing recognisable to me'. She was so startled that she forgot to speak to people in another car that pulled into the layby to watch the UFO. Her report was passed to a secretive branch of the MoD, DI55, that was responsible for the investigation of UFO reports deemed to have possible defence significance. The DI55 UFO officer asked RAF Watton to examine radar film from the relevant date and time. They identified the object as nothing more unusual than a Boeing 720, which had diverted from Gatwick and landed at Stansted airport at 9.15 having crossed the A12 ten miles southwest of Colchester. In his response to the RAF Group Captain, the intelligence officer said: 'As you know, Stansted is not far from Colchester and on that day the in-bound flight pattern was towards the southwest and passed directly over the point your daughter gave'. He added: 'These reports interest me in that they raise physiological and psychological factors which are beyond my competence to investigate'. DEFE 24/1211; DEFE 31/164

At 7.10pm on New Years' Eve 1978, hundreds across the British Isles saw a spectacular fiery object moving northwest to southeast in the clear night sky. Many of them were outdoors en route to New Year parties, making this one of the best multi-witness sightings ever reported in the UK. The MoD received 104 separate reports and many others were logged by the Civil Aviation Authority and civilian UFO associations like BUFORA and Contact UK. Among the reports logged by the RAF were these: a Manchester man described the phenomena as 'cigar-shaped, very bright, especially the tail, with seven lighted windows'; in Bradford it was 'similar to an old German V2 rocket... flying at 1,000 ft'; in Newmarket it was 'train-shaped, 120ft long, tapering in front with 40 plus bright lights all the way along the side'. This flying object was also tracked by the RAF's early warning station at Fylingdales on the North York Moors. They identified it as the re-entry into Earth's atmosphere of the booster rocket that had launched the Russian satellite Cosmos 1068 into orbit on 26 December. The rocket had burnt up over northern Europe, scattering pieces of debris across western Germany. But even after the facts were published, some who had witnessed the spectacular incident remained dissatisfied. One of these was a retired RAF serviceman, who wrote to his former employers to describe his own sighting from Southwick Road, Sunderland. He said the object appeared oval in shape with 'a large cone of light' to the rear, as bright as a car headlight seen head-on. It was moving northwest at the approximate speed and height of a light aircraft and made no sound. In response, the MoD said 'there is nothing that can be added to the statement already made which explained that the incident was caused by the decay of space debris into the Earth's atmosphere'. DEFE 24/1212; DEFE 24/1552

Continued.

appeared to have the approximate speed of a light aircraft, at the same height, and moved in a straight line, parellel to the earth. and horizon. The weather at the time was fresh and clear with cloud formations of ensignificant size. /

Breifly a description of the object is as follows. The leading part appeared to be of a shape between eliptical and round, .oval, the rear part being what appeared to be large cone of light. The lead part was of about a ½ pence peice size, held at arms length, and the rear being about the length of perhaps 11 or 12 times that of the width of the first part. Please see diagram. The brightness was of that of a car head light when veiwed head on, very bright and impossible to miss, it was a white light. The object made no noise whatso ever.

Diagram.



As I was for 5 years in the R.A.F serving at R.A.F STAXTON WOLD, early warning radar, and was a witness to various things i.e. meteors and re-entry of space debris, I find it difficult to accept current explantions for this occurance, and would be grateful if on further investigation you could enform me

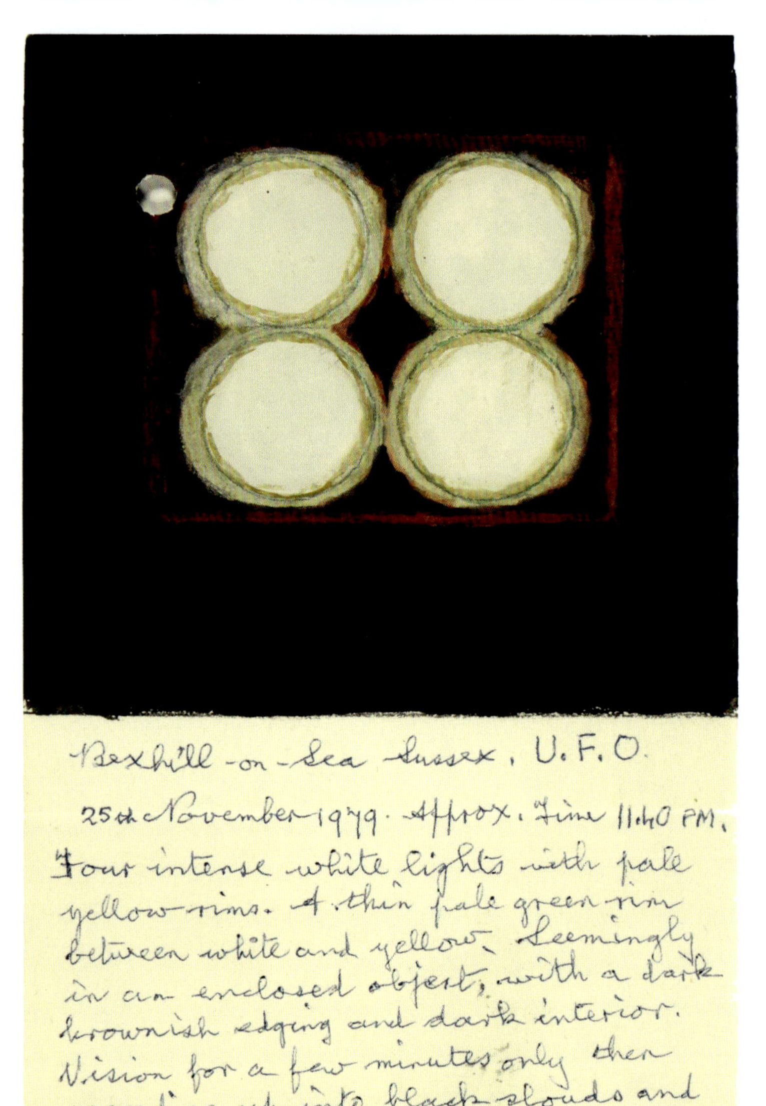

Bexhill-on-Sea Sussex, U.F.O.

25th November 1979. Approx. Time 11.40 PM.
Four intense white lights with pale
yellow rims. A thin pale green rim
between white and yellow. Seemingly
in an enclosed object, with a dark
brownish edging and dark interior.
Vision for a few minutes only then
receding up into black clouds and
out to sea.
Seen from our flat window when
drawing curtains prior to retiring to
bed. Television completely ruined by
electric disturbance at the time,
both sound, colour and vision
out of focus. Advice given out
from Hastings. "This is beyond our
control, do not attempt to alter sets"
This trouble had been on for at least
an hour before we decided to
finish.                    P.T.O.

One dark night in November 1979 Percy Mercer was watching TV in his flat at Bexhill-on-Sea, Sussex, when the picture was ruined by 'electrical interference'. One hour later, near midnight, when the 84-year-old went to draw the curtains his wife pointed to 'a strange object in the sky' over the English Channel. Mr Mercer, who had served in the Royal Flying Corps during the First World War, immediately fetched his glasses to help him focus on the object. As he watched, it receded upwards into a band of heavy cloud, before it vanished seawards towards France. He made a very quick pencil sketch of the UFO and, next day, produced a coloured drawing that he sent to the MoD in London. He described the object as 'four intense white lights with pale yellow rims' separated by a pale green rim, all enclosed within a dark box-shaped structure. In a letter sent in response to Mr Mercer's report, UFO desk officer Miss G.J. Jamieson said 'the sole aim of the Ministry of Defence with regard to UFO reports is to establish any possible defence implications'. She said no report had ever been identified as a threat and 'simple explanations are found for the great majority...the most common single source being aircraft or the lights of aircraft seen under unusual meteorological conditions'. DEFE 24/1913

*next spread* —▷-



An estate agent called the police after he and his wife spotted a silver coloured UFO from their home in Durrington, near Worthing in Sussex. In their statement, dated 11 May 1981, the couple said the object was 'silver on top and matt black on the bottom with alternate blocks of each colour in a band around the visible circumference of the object'. After examining the object through binoculars he noticed a second identical UFO that appeared at the same point in the sky. Both travelled west until they disappeared from sight. He drew a sketch of the second object and took four or five photographs of it using an Olympus 35mm camera fitted with a 200mm lens and Kodachrome 64 ASA film. 'I have held a private pilot's licence for over ten years and in my years of flying and contact with things aeronautical, have not come across any similar object,' he added. DEFE 24/1513

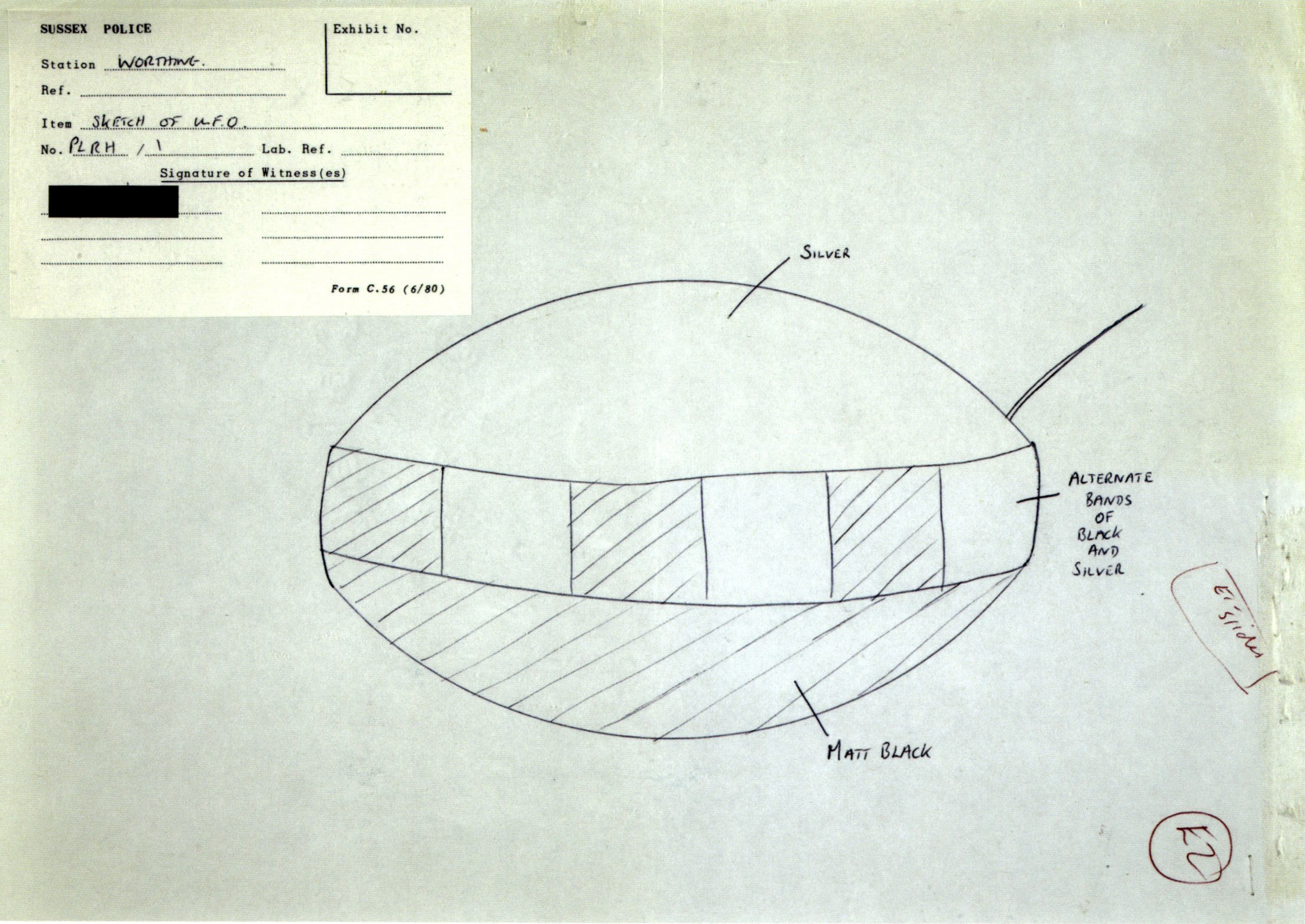
SILVER
ALTERNATE
BANDS
OF
BLACK
AND
SILVER
MATT BLACK

WED 8"/OCT/1981

SEEN FLYING OVER
HILINGBURY TRADING ESTATE
BRTN.
BETWEEN 9.30 10² P.M.

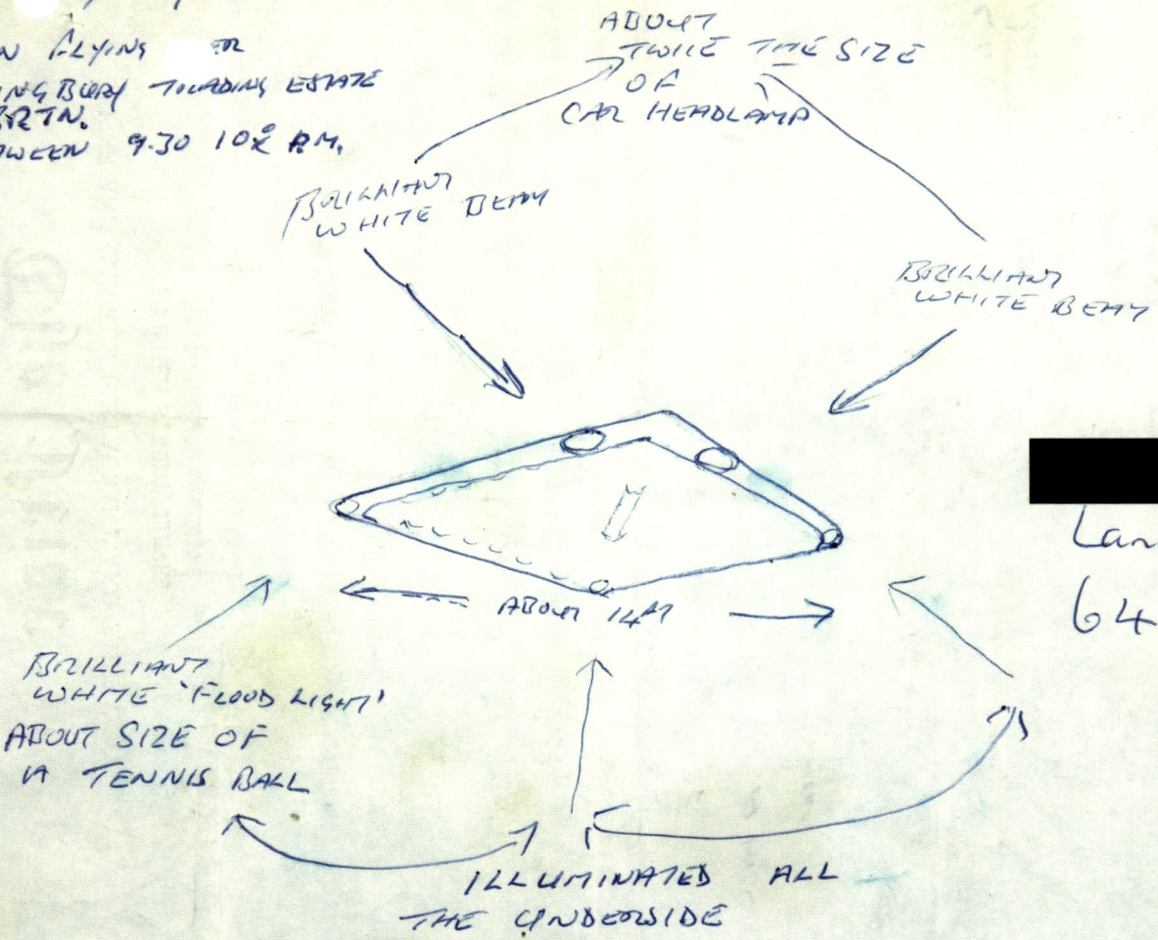

ABOUT
TWICE THE SIZE
OF
CAR HEADLAMP

BRILLIANT
WHITE BEAM

BRILLIANT
WHITE BEAM

Lancing
64827.

ABOUT 14M

BRILLIANT
WHITE 'FLOOD LIGHT'
ABOUT SIZE OF
A TENNIS BALL

ILLUMINATED ALL
THE UNDERSIDE

One afternoon in November 1981 a policeman in Lewes, Sussex, was approached by the owner of a fish n' chip shop who said he 'wished to report a sighting of a UFO'. In his account, handed to the police, he said he was driving home from work on the evening of 28 October 1981, when his wife pointed out a 'brilliant white light' suspended in the sky as they approached the top of Coldean Lane in Brighton. As they drove further, reaching the crest of a second hill, the silent object flew directly overhead towards the east and then veered north. In his statement, attached to a sketch of the UFO, he says that on the second occasion 'we [could] see four separate lights, two bright headlights, two side-lights and what appeared to look like a conventional aircraft on a forward approach. It passed by and over my side of the car and I opened the car window and had a clear view of what I have drawn overleaf'. DEFE 24/1513

*next spread* —▷

## 1981

This colour felt-tip sketch of a UFO was handed to Staffordshire police in July 1981 by a 38-year-old mother-of-three from Wheaton Aston, near Cannock. She described the object as 'oval in shape with a dome, turquoise blue and glowing'. She was with a friend in the living room of her home at 10.45 pm on 30 July when they both saw the object, moving slowly north to south towards Wolverhampton. DEFE 24/1513

1st stage

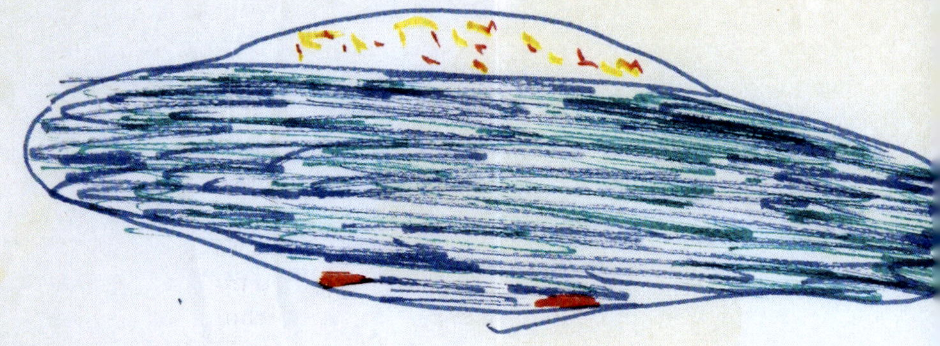

2nd stage
middle appeared to
disappear

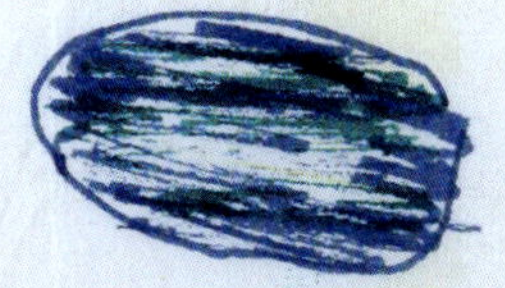

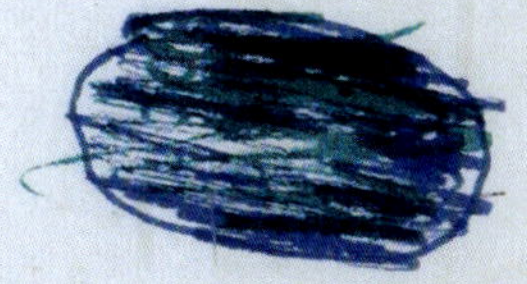

A motorist from Leeds, Yorkshire, sent this sketch attached to a letter: 'At about 2.45 on the morning of October 15th I was driving south along the A1 near RAF Leeming when what I can only describe as a UFO nearly landed on the A1 just in front of me. As I was driving I had noticed a red light in the sky getting nearer and nearer very quickly. At first I thought it must be a plane but as it got closer I was startled to see what appeared to be a flying parallelogram with red and white lights set diagonally. I then saw two white lights as it tilted... I dipped my headlights, it just hovered [and] getting a bit startled, I put the car headlights on, it very slowly veered to its right, my left, directly overhead at very low height and vanished in a field behind some trees'. The driver heard no noise and was certain it was not a plane, glider or balloon. Wing Commander Barrett of RAF Leeming checked and found there was no military aircraft flying in the vicinity of Leeming at the time. 'However, a HS748 operated by Dan Air Services Ltd, landed at RAF Leeming [at 2 am]. Although the timing differs from that in the report, the description almost fits a civilian airliner fitted with navigation and anti-collision lights. The approach path was parallel to and very close to the A1. I suspect this was the aircraft he saw despite the comments in his letter'. DEFE 24/1513

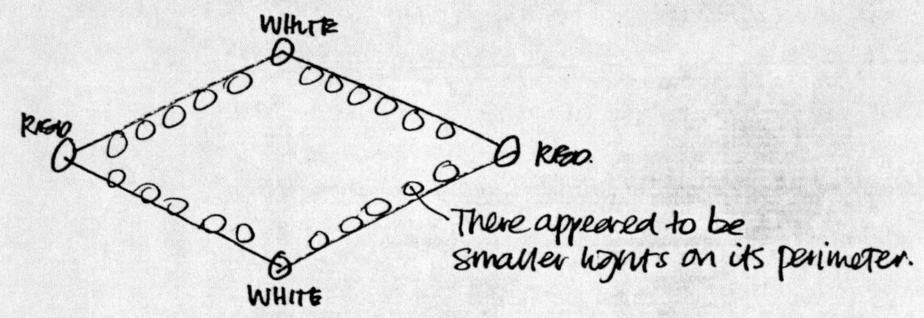


There appeared to be
smaller lights on its perimeter.

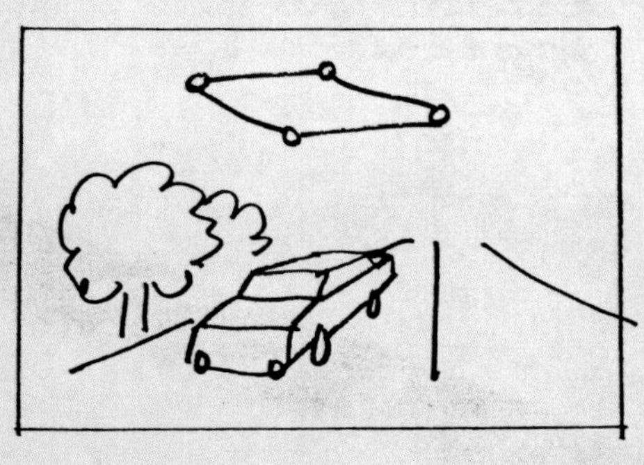

In the summer of 1983 the mystery of the 'cornfield circles' was all over the pages of Britain's tabloid newspapers. When a formation of five circles appeared at Westbury, Wiltshire, in July the *Daily Express* published a dramatic aerial photograph of the phenomenon alongside an image from Steven Spielberg's movie ET – *The Extra Terrestrial,* released earlier in the year. On 11 July the MoD's UFO desk received a letter from a correspondent in Leigh, Lancashire, who said he believed it was unlikely that human beings could have created the corn circles. He said it was more likely they were result of a landing made by a 'vertical landing and take-off aircraft' powered by reversible fans and equipped with tripod landing gear, similar to those used by NASA's lunar module. He followed up his letter with a large A3 drawing of a 'negative boundary aircraft' that fitted the description of the marks in the cornfields. This was designed by him in the 1950s and submitted to the government. 'No one was interested!,' he wrote, '"Someone" was, but who?' In reply, the MoD said they believed the crop circles were caused by 'some kind of natural phenomena'. DEFE 24/1517

by a lunar module landing on
the moon.
3 This leaves an internal combustion
powered aircraft. Sketched below
is how I picture it!



4 Telescopic
legs fitted
with "Air" Ball wheels.
(Retracted, they could
land on air or water)
"Amphibious"!

Engine
probably "silenced"

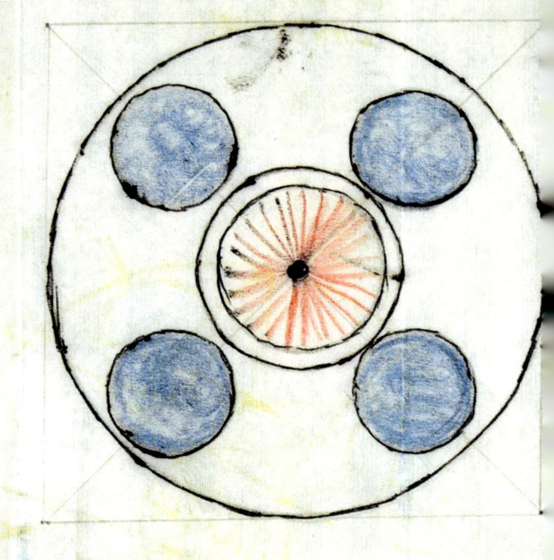

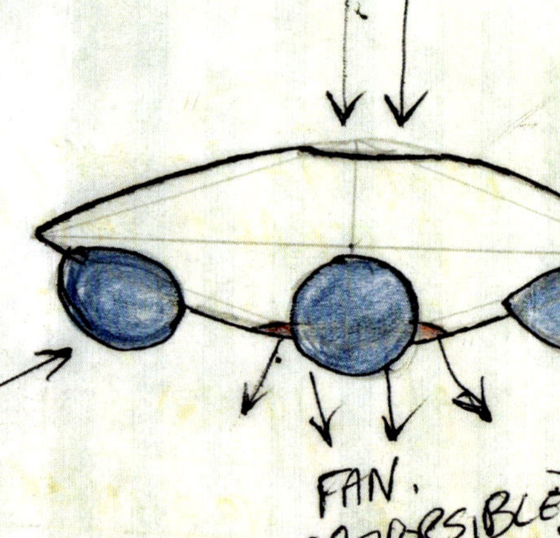Helium
Filled
Ball
Feet.
FAN.
(REVERSIBLE).

LEIGH
LANCASHIRE

HELIUM
FILLED
BALL FEET

motor
& reversible
FAN

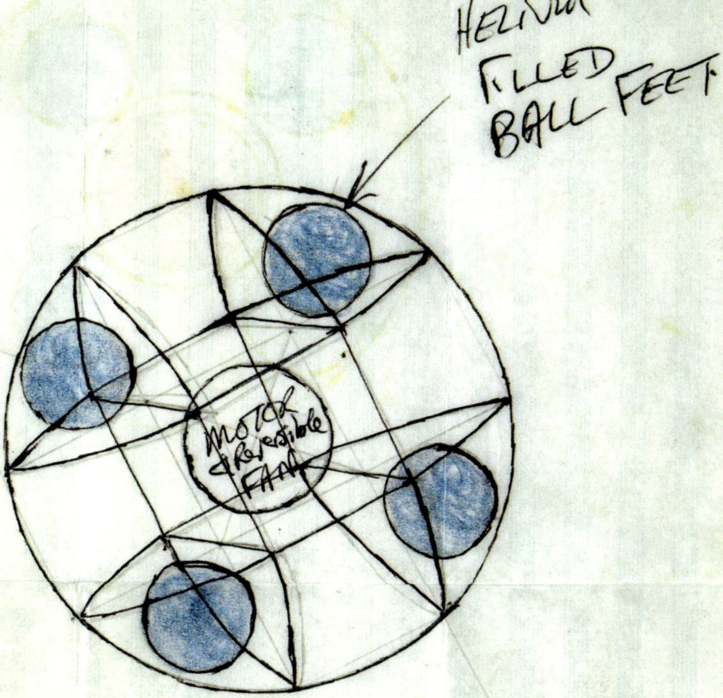

NEGATIVE BOUANCY
AIRCRAFT. (Amphibious)
Designed by me in
the 1950's

NO ONE was INTERESTED!

"someone" was, but who?

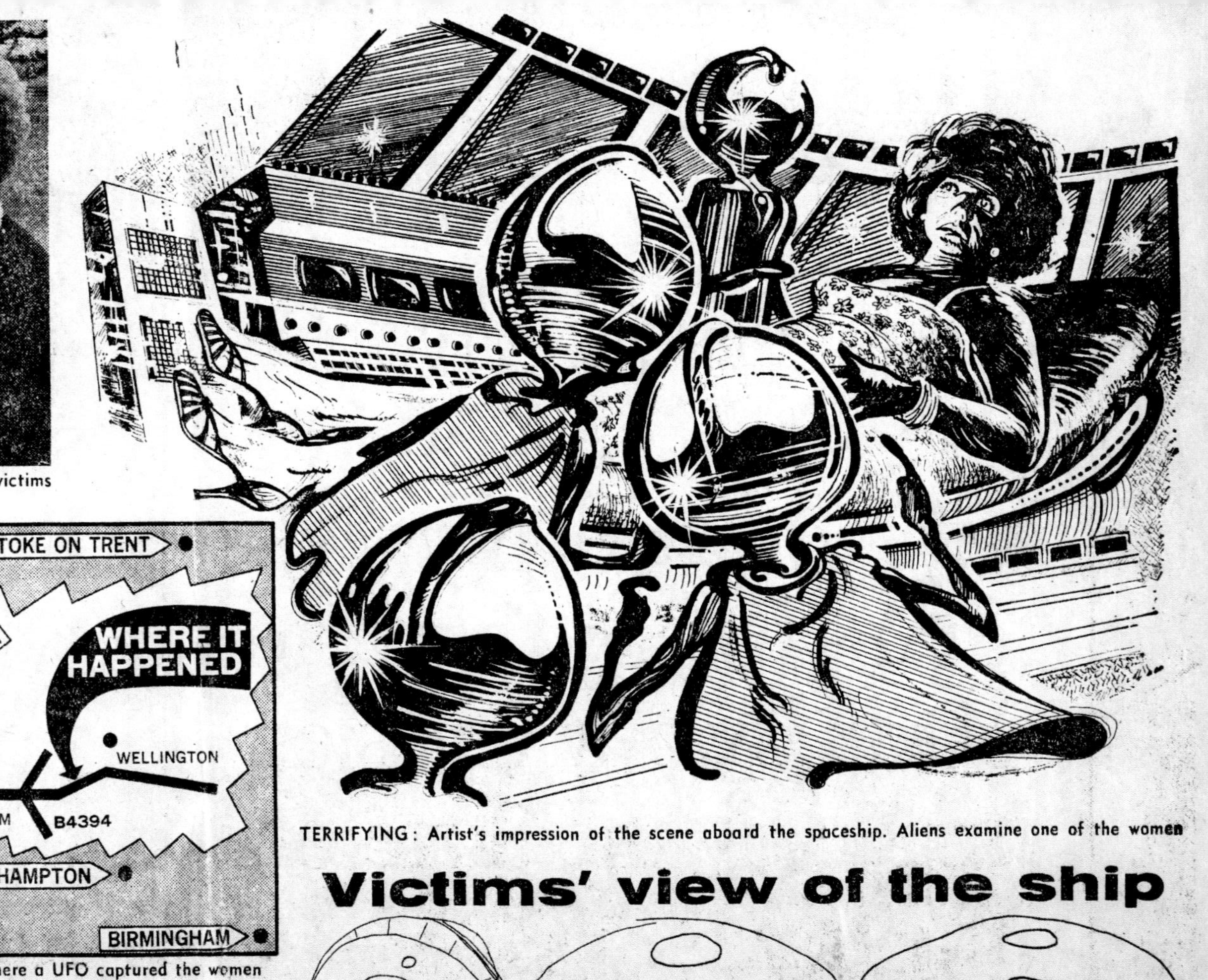


...nd Rosemary, UFO victims

THE SPOT where a UFO captured the women

TERRIFYING: Artist's impression of the scene aboard the spaceship. Aliens examine one of the women

# Victims' view of the ship

UNCANNY: Under hypnosis the three women produced similar drawings of the spaceship's underside

relaxed and they feel friendly, I like them."

She adds: "I am floating again. I can see the car. Everything has gone black.

"I'm in the car now. Val and Viv are there with me. Viv's got her foot down hard on the accelerator.

"I feel I'm floating," she says "I'm being drawn up. The car is being taken up." Sobbing, she adds: "I can't see the road any more. I see a white cloud.

"I'm on my own. I can see the door of the UFO open. It is round. I'm looking through the car wind-

The phrase 'close encounters of the third kind' was coined in 1972 by the astronomer Dr J. Allen Hynek, who advised the USAF Project Blue Book, to classify UFO experiences that involved the observation of alien creatures. It was later adopted as the title for Steven Spielberg's blockbuster film of that name, released in 1978, based on the theme of contact with friendly aliens. But during the 1980s bizarre and terrifying stories began to emerge from sincere witnesses who claimed they had been forcibly abducted by the occupants of UFOs who subjected them to intrusive medical examinations before returning them to Earth. The MoD received several reports of this kind and the files contain letters and newspaper cuttings on what the press called 'alien abductions'. This artist's impression was published in *The News of the World* on 5 June 1983 under the headline 'Encounter at the Shamrock Café'. It told how three young women had inexplicably lost a period of time after they spotted a series of strange lights in the sky whilst driving home along the A5 from a night out in Shrewsbury, Shropshire. Seeking answers for their 'missing time' the trio turned to regression hypnosis. All three were regressed separately and told similar stories of being lifted from their car into a craft where they were examined by ugly creatures four feet in height with deep-set dark eyes and thin arms. MoD offered no explanations for these experiences but in 1996, when questioned by a correspondent about their lack of concern, UFO desk officer Kerry Philpott responded: 'Abduction is a criminal offence and as such is a matter for the civil police'. DEFE 24/1517; DEFE 24/1943/1

In October 1983 pensioner Alfred Burtoo told the *Aldershot News* he had been taken on board a flying saucer by little green men who landed on the towpath of the Basingstoke Canal. Mr Burtoo was out night-fishing, accompanied by his dog Tiny, when he saw 'a bright light in the sky' approaching them. Mr Burtoo, then 77, said he was approached by two four-foot high 'forms' dressed in green coveralls. Their faces were covered by dark visors. One beckoned to him and he followed them up a flight of steps into the object that was made of 'a kind of burnished aluminium'. Burtoo said he wasn't afraid, 'I was more curious than anything'. One of the crew, who communicated in an odd sing-song voice, asked him to stand under an amber lamp. Then one of the aliens asked his age, to which he replied: 'I shall be 78 next birthday'. Soon afterwards, 'he said to me, "You can go. You are too old and too infirm for our purpose"'. After leaving the UFO he watched it leave, then carried on fishing. He later told his wife Marjorie and a neighbour about the encounter but did not report it officially because 'he did not think people would believe him'. Mr Burtoo decided to talk to the media after the *News of the World* published the sensational account of USAF servicemen who saw a UFO land near RAF Woodbridge, in Suffolk. In December 1985 UFOlogist Timothy Good sent a copy of Mr Burtoo's story and his drawings of the UFO and aliens to the MoD, noting that 'the witness... seems thoroughly honest to me, and would be glad to talk to your people if necessary'. Mr Burtoo died in 1986. DEFE 24/1925/1

(SKETCHES BY ██████████)

OVERALL WITH ABOUT 45 FEET
INTERNAL LIGHT ON OTHER SIDE OF HERE
EXTERNAL LIGHT FROM HERE ALL AROUND
HIGH TO TOP OF STEPS ABOUT 12 TO 15 FEET
HIGHT ABOUT 18 FEET FROM GROUND

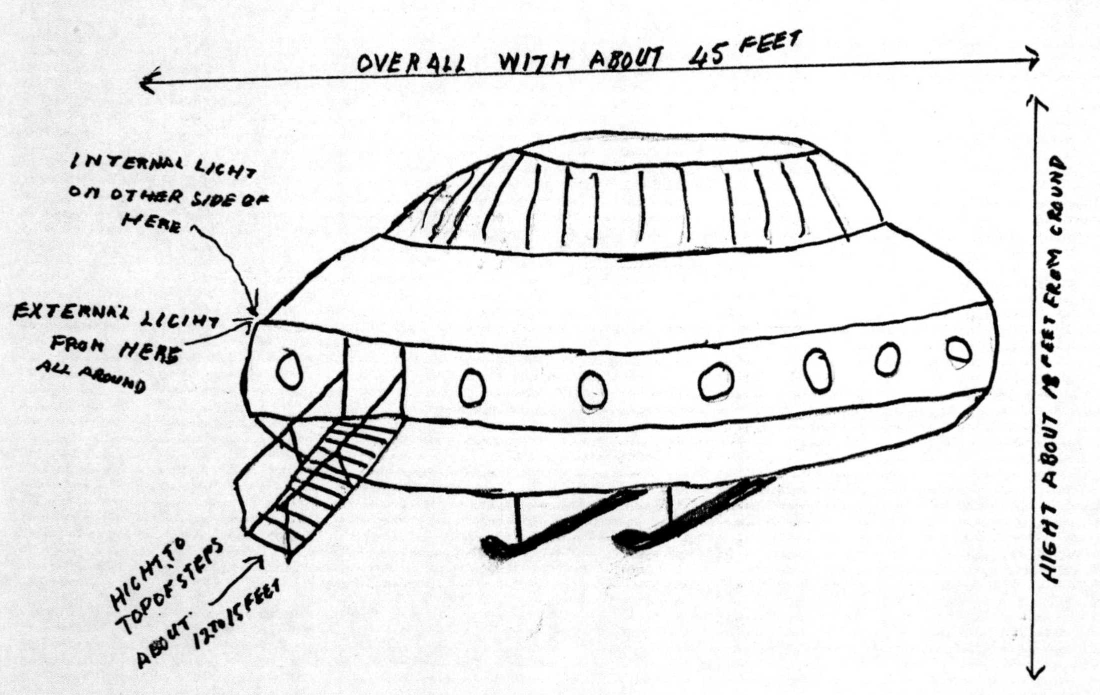

Late one night in April 1984, a group of puzzled police officers gathered in the garden of a house in Stanmore, north London, to watch a rotating, multi-coloured circular UFO in the sky. One of them, PC Dick Milthorp, 22, drew this sketch of the stationary object that he watched through a pair of binoculars for more than one hour. It was submitted to New Scotland Yard who passed it to the Ministry of Defence. The MoD files reveal they were called by Miss Terri West who spotted a bright light in the sky at 9.45 pm when she opened the back door of her home on Belmont Lane to let the dog out. She called to her neighbour Ruth Novelli and, after watching the UFO for some time, they screamed as a 'blinding white ball with a trail' appeared to flash above and behind the rotating object. When the police arrived at 10.45 pm the 'bright flickering' object was still visible. The group spent another hour skywatching. In his statement, PC Milthorp said the women pointed towards a flashing light at 45 degrees elevation in the northeastern sky towards Mill Hill. He described it as 'circular in the middle with what appeared to be a dome on top and underneath… there were blue lights around the middle and red/pink lights on the extreme right of the middle'. Intermittent flashes of coloured light could be seen emanating from this object. Their report describes how the police watched this UFO for 'an hour and during this time [it] moved erratically from side to side, up and down and to and fro, not venturing far from the original position'. Astronomer Ian Ridpath checked the directions and timing of the sighting using a computer programme. He believes the UFO was most likely to be the bright blue-white star, Vega, the fifth-brightest star in the night sky. This was visible at a lower altitude than was estimated by the witnesses. In his view the sketch of the Saturn-shaped object was the product of 'an optical distortion' that can occur when a twinkling star is viewed through binoculars. The bright 'flash' reported could have been a meteor from the Lyrid shower that peaks on 22 April and radiates from the same direction of the sky as Vega. When the file on the Stanmore UFO was opened by The National Archives in 2008 one of the witnesses, Ruth Novelli, was interviewed by the *Daily Mail*. She claimed that shortly after she reported the sighting a black car that contained three swarthy Italian-looking men, dressed in black suits, arrived at her home. She was out, but a neighbour spotted the strange visitors. Were these well-dressed UFOlogists or the dreaded Men In Black? DEFE 24/1925/1

Unidentified object as seen by [REDACTED] and [REDACTED] through binoculars at approximately 11pm Dated 26TH April 1984.

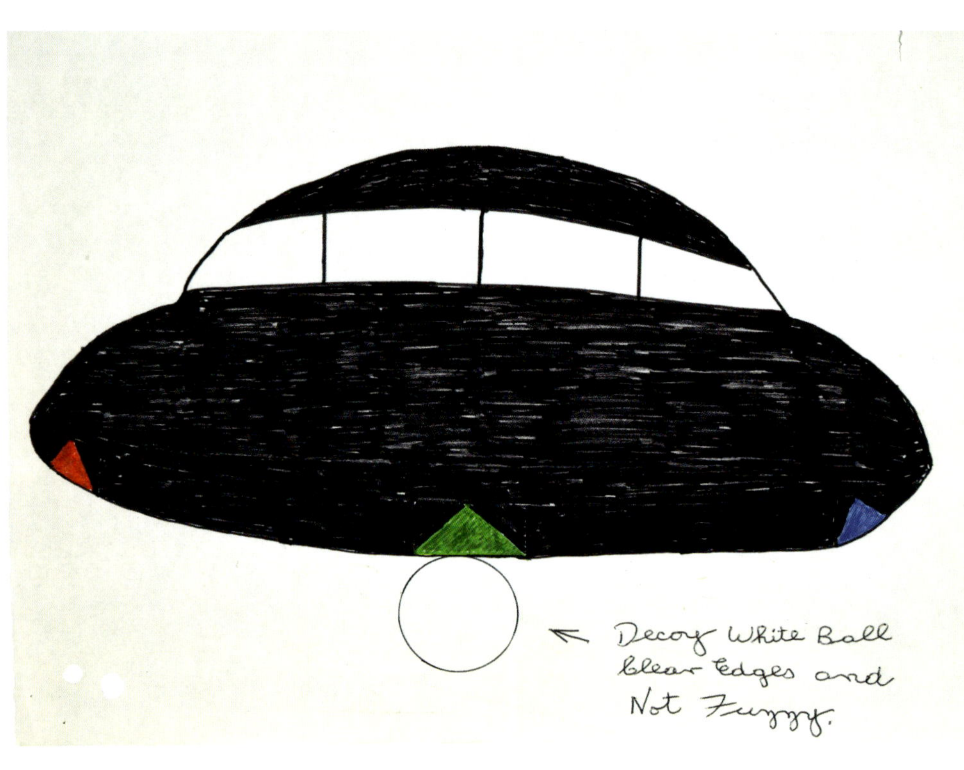
← Decoy White Ball
Clear Edges and
Not Fuzzy.

This drawing depicts a UFO over Lough Neagh in Northern Ireland sighted by a letter-writer who believed the area was a target for extra-terrestrial visitations. 'May I point out to you that this object is a decoy?' his letter informed MoD. 'The main object is just above this craft, it is around 20 feet in diameter and about 9 feet high it has a brilliant lit cabin. It uses as a camouflage invisibility if they are caught off guard. It works just like switching an electric light on and off. I found this out one February night of this year [1985] when I was tracking two moving white lights near Lurgan Golf Course with a friend. Suddenly I saw this round object above me about 50 feet up hovering, making no noise. I flashed my torch at it... at once it flashed on this football size white ball beneath it and made a dive towards us... it was then I saw this brilliant lit cabin as it was just going over our heads. The main object just vanished only the glowing white ball could be seen. Later that night I photographed two white revolving lights that seemed to be attached [to] two invisible objects sitting on the golf course'. His letter added: 'These creatures are not human. They are Fallen Angels'. DEFE 24/1925/1

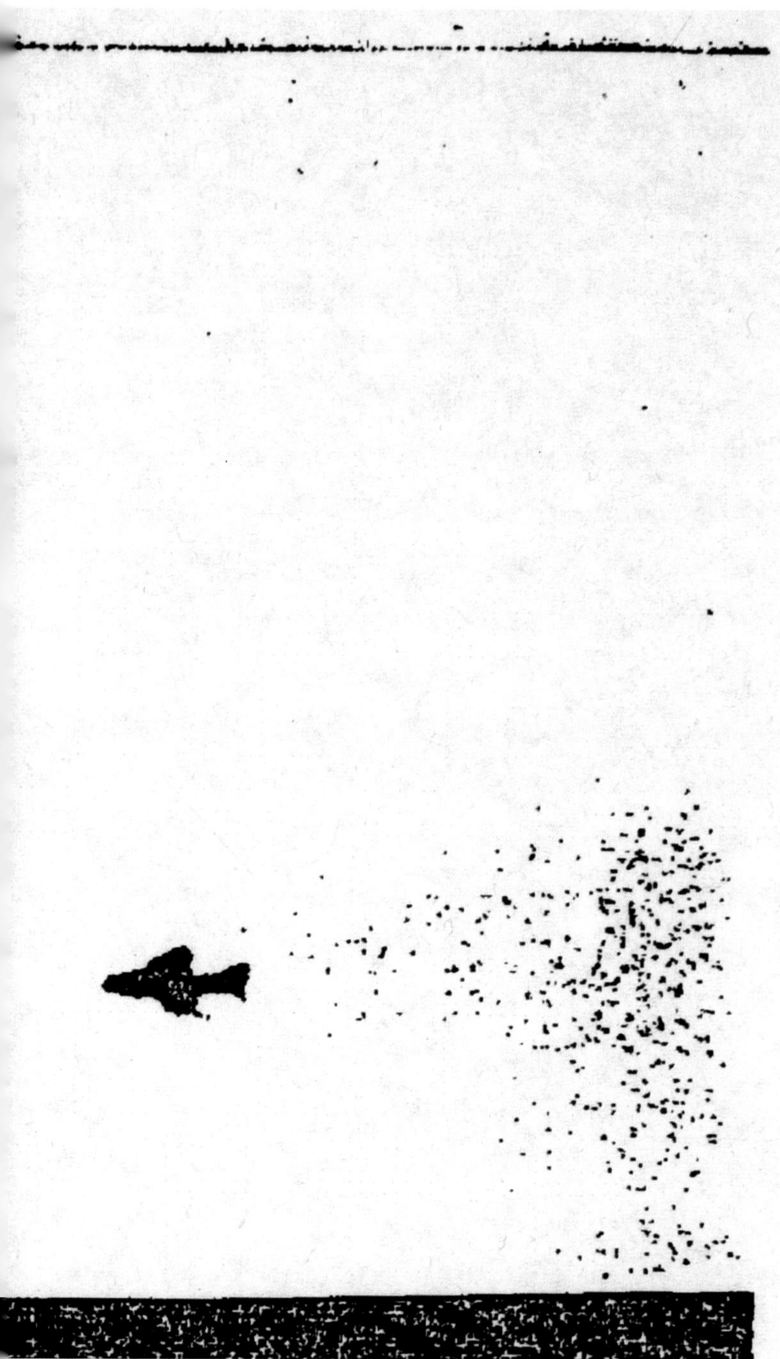

◁— *previous spread*

## 1990

This curious image of a dark, diamond-shaped object in the sky shadowed by a tiny jet aircraft is all that remains of what one MoD desk officer has called 'the most compelling UFO photo I've ever seen'. This photocopied print was taken from a set of colour photographs that some MoD officials suspected might show a top secret USAF spy-plane operating in UK airspace. According to the file, the originals were taken by two men walking near the Scottish village of Calvine, near the A9, around 9pm on 4 August 1990. They said the UFO hovered for about ten minutes 'before ascending vertically upwards at high speed'. During this time they also saw RAF jet aircraft making a number of low-level passes. Afterwards the negatives were sent to the Scottish *Daily Record* newspaper who passed them to the MoD but did not publish the story. According to the MoD files, after detailed analysis the ministry's photo intelligence experts identified not one but two RAF Harriers visible on the image. But adding further to the mystery, their own inquiries found 'there is no record of Harriers operating in the area at the time at which the photographs are alleged to have been taken'. The file reveals the original negatives were returned to the photographer, but two years later DI55 asked another branch, 'to produce line drawings of [the] object with size and dimensions where possible'. What happened to these detailed drawings is not explained by the surviving files. Nick Pope said a poster-sized enlarged version of one photograph was kept on the wall of the office when he took on the post of UFO desk officer from Owen Hartop in 1991. Pope told the *Daily Record* in 2012 that it was later removed by his head of division. 'I suspect that certain people thought that this was some secret prototype aircraft, a next-generation stealth that maybe nobody should be seeing', he said. DEFE 31/180

*next spread* —▷

**1994**

A self-described amateur artist produced this striking drawing of a UFO he saw and photographed as it hovered above the Craigluscar Reservoir, near Dunfermline in Fife, on the afternoon of 15 February 1994. According to his typewritten account, sent to MoD, he had visited the beauty spot to take photographs 'to assist me in producing a painting of the reservoir'. Whilst looking eastwards, 'I became aware of what I can only describe as a kind of humming noise, such as that from high voltage power lines'. He continued: 'I also felt very uneasy, and turned slowly towards the reservoir'. High in the air and moving towards him was a disc-shaped object, but despite holding his Chinon SLR camera in his hands, he felt unable to take a shot. 'I later realised that I must have been looking at whatever it was for more than fifteen minutes. The craft came close enough for me to see that it was definitely metallic and had several points of diffused light on its underside, inside a darker coloured 'rim'. As the craft began to move away, all sense of the feelings which had stayed my hand, disappeared. I raised my camera and took two photographs. The craft's acceleration was phenomenal – by the time I'd wound the film on between the two shots, it was a mere dot in the sky to the west'. At this close point there was no noise at all. In his summary of the story, prepared for the head of the UFO desk, Nick Pope said 'he appeared genuine... did not appear to know anything about UFOs, and aside from his own experience, expressed no interest in the subject. It seems to me that this case is either a hoax, or something very genuine indeed'. DEFE 24/2048/1

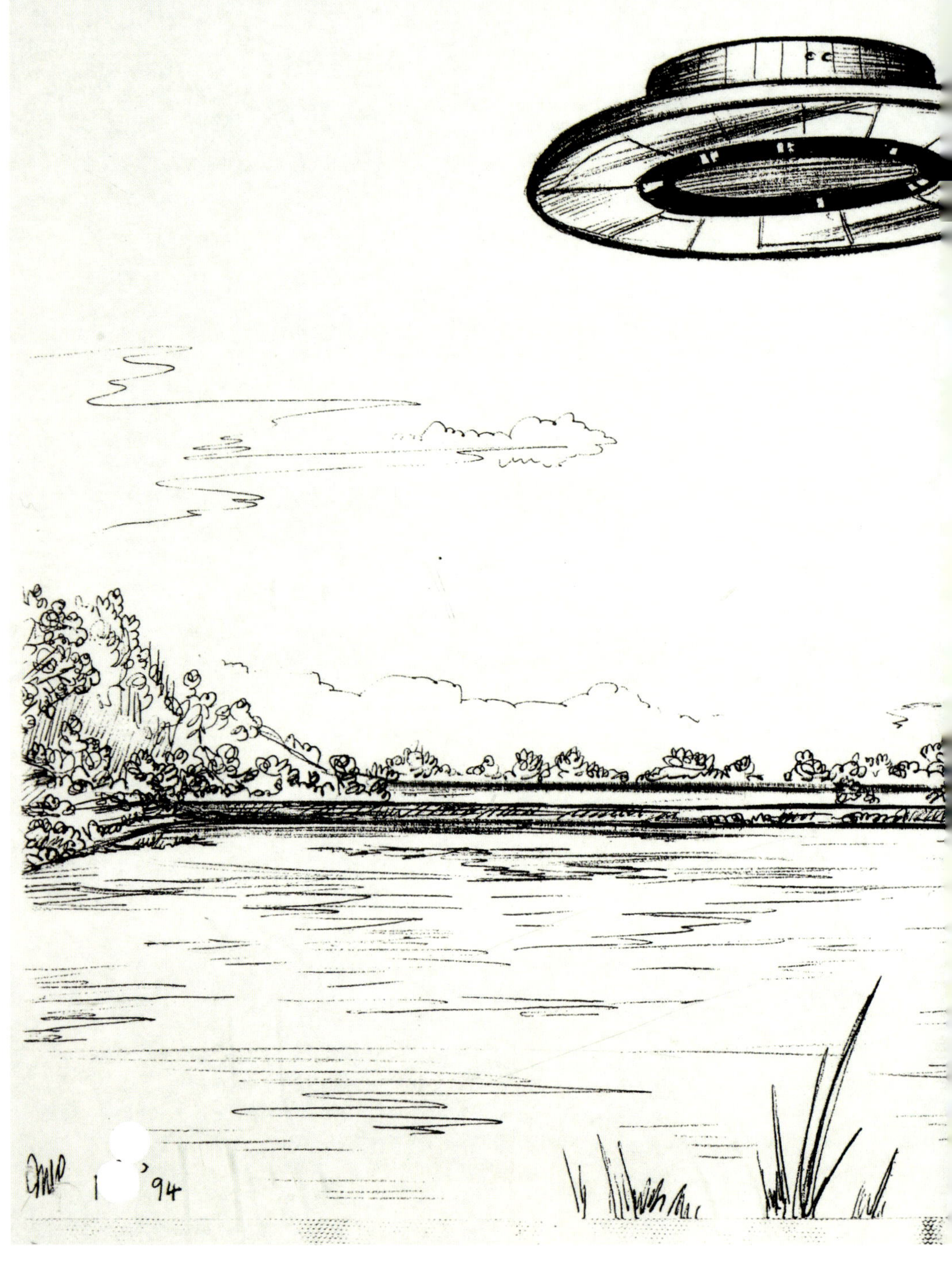

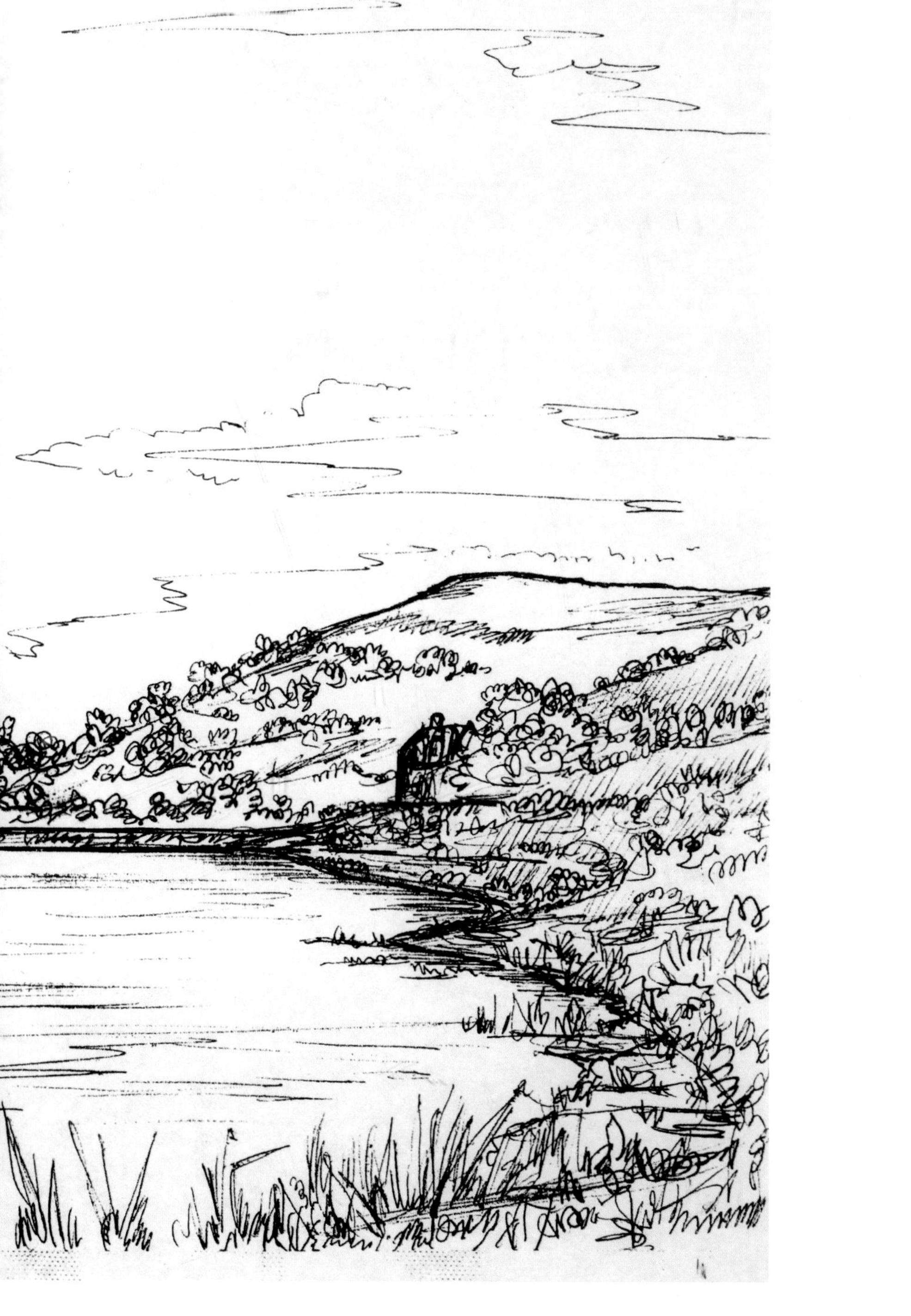

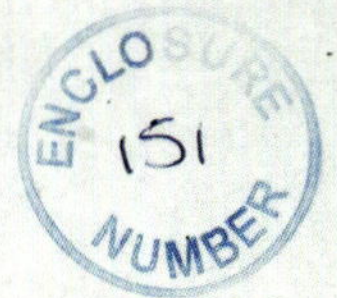

ANNEX A TO
ORDER NO 16 TO
COC ORDERS
DATED 26 JAN 95

5 Oct 97

## REPORT ON AN UNIDENTIFIED FLYING OBJECT

1.  **Date, Time and Duration of Sighting:** 0819 5 P.A. OCT 97 ..........
........ 5 MINUTES ..............................................

2.  **Description of Object** (No of objects, size, shape, colour, brightness,
sound, smell, etc): ONE BALL OF FIRE WITH TAIL ........
ORANGE COLOURED ...................................................

3.  **Exact Position when Observed** (Geographical Location, Indoors or
Outdoors, Stationary or Moving): CAMP MUIR 2 MILES FROM ....
KIRRIELTON NR COUPAR ANGUS .......................................

4.  **How Observed** (Naked Eye, Binoculars, Still or Movie Camera/VCR):
........
.... NAKED EYE ...................................................

5.  **Direction in which Object was First Seen** (Possibly with Reference to a
Landmark): WEST (ABOVE PERTH) ...............................
................................................................

6.  **Angle of Sight** (Estimated Heights are Unreliable): 30 DEGREES
ABOVE HORIZON .............................................

7.  **Distance** (With Reference to a Landmark if Possible): FAR AWAY
ABOUT 15 MILES ..............................................

8.  **Movements** (Changes in 6, 7 & 8 may be better than Estimates of Heading
and Speed): DROPPING DOWN .................................
................................................................
................................................................

9.  **Weather:** (Moving Clouds, Visibility) CLOUDY .........................

## 1995

Since 1954, the British government have relied upon a standard questionnaire to gather basic information from members of the public who wished to make an official report about a sighting of an unidentified flying object. The original Air Ministry form was based upon a template used by investigators for the US Air Force's UFO project, Blue Book. During the 1960s the Ministry of Defence updated the forms and distributed copies to RAF stations, air traffic control centres and police stations. When a member of the public called to report a sighting, personnel would obtain basic data such as time, duration, angle of sight, location and weather conditions that might help to provide an explanation. But the restrictive format of these categories left little space for officials to enter some of the more unusual details supplied by UFO witnesses. There are also occasional examples in the files of what one official described as 'uncomplimentary comments' made by staff about people who called to report frivolous observations, for example of 'two objects that looked like stars' or 'a dot in the sky that did not look like an airplane'. On this form a RAF duty officer, with a sense of humour, has added an improvised UFO/alien cartoon to a run-of-the-mill report of lights in the sky over a Scottish town. The forms used by MoD were withdrawn in December 2009 when the MoD closed its UFO desk and asked police and air traffic control centres not to send any further sighting reports to them. DEFE 24/1989/1

*next spread* →

## 1998

This drawing of a UFO producing a crop circle was sent to Secretariat Air Staff 2 (the UFO desk) in November 1998 from a correspondent in Oxfordshire. His letter said: 'I have developed contact with these craft and their energy forces but unfortunately the designs I am perceiving are too complex for me to draw... these include anti-gravitational fields that allow the craft to access time'. In her response the desk officer, Kerry Philpott, said: 'There is no evidence to suggest that crop circles are caused by anything of military concern and the MoD does not, therefore, investigate reported sightings or carry out any research into them'. DEFE/1999/1

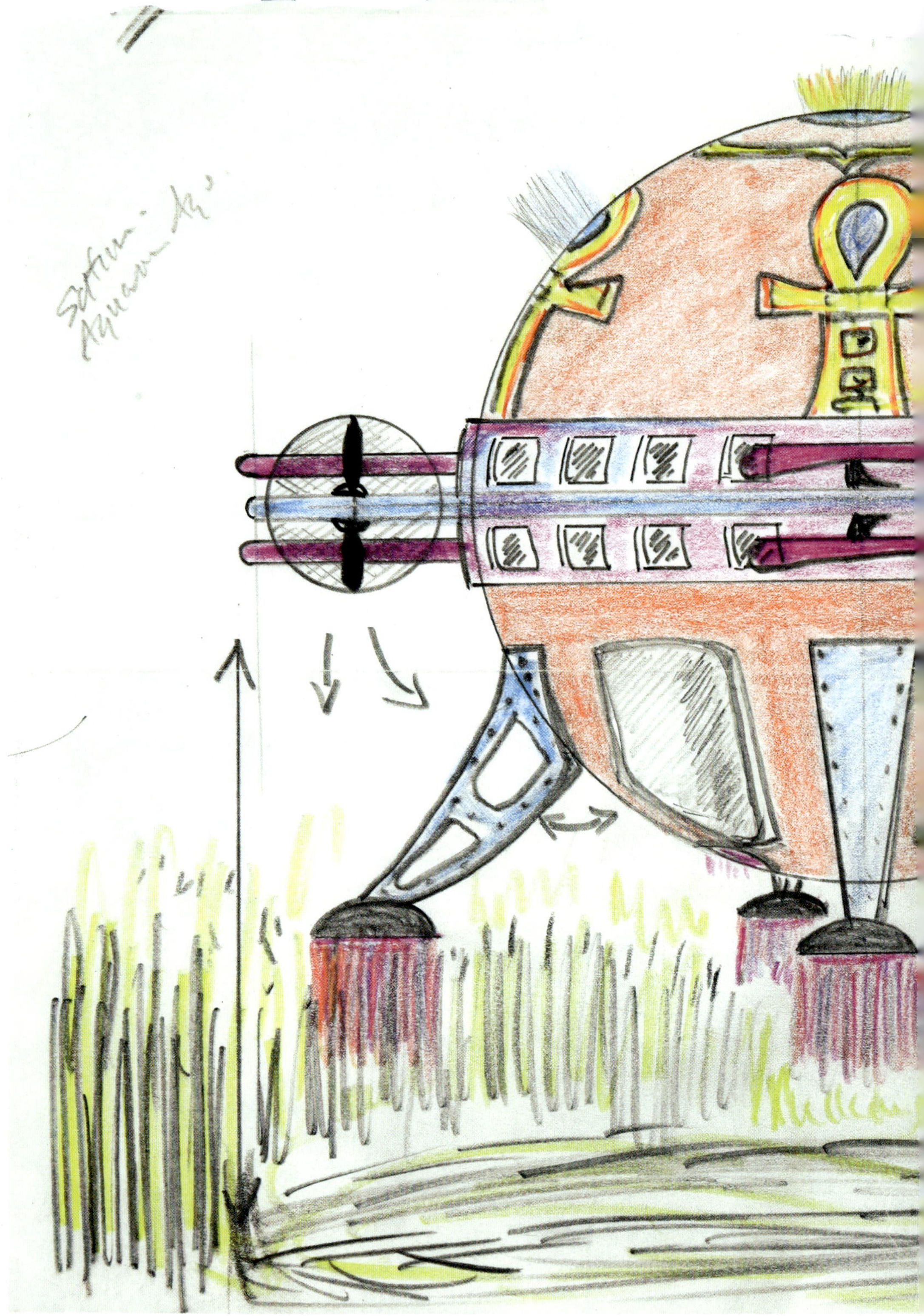

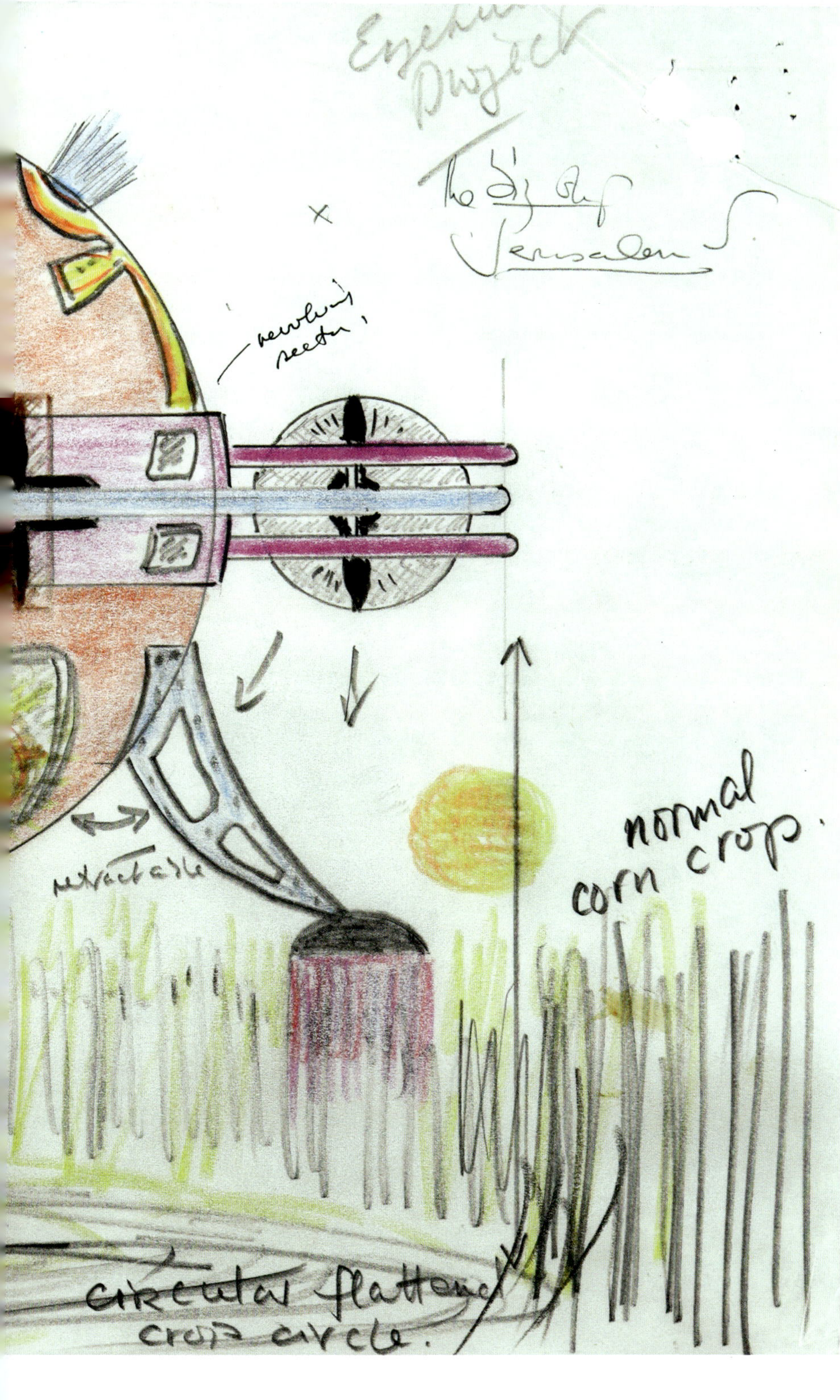

Eschaton
Project
The Big Rip
Jerusalem
newborn
sector
retractable
normal
corn crop
circular flattened
crop circle.

Since the 1980s one of the most common UFO types reported in the USA and UK has been a huge, triangular shaped object that is dark in colour and carries powerful lights. These are often noticed by observers before the body of the object comes into view. In this case a resident of Stroud, Gloucestershire sent his MP, David Drew, a detailed account and a diagram showing a 'black triangle' that he observed flying above a ridge of hills in the southern Cotswolds one night in September 2000. He was out on an evening stroll at 9.30 when he was surprised to see a strange object looming up over the skyline. 'This was no ordinary aircraft as it was black all over with no tail section... and it had three *very* powerful beams of light, lighting up ahead of the aircraft – all three lights emanated from underneath the aircraft from dome-like globes and were set in a triangular shape. The only other lights were extremely small red lights on the extreme tips of each wing, the wing's [sic] of which were *extremely* long and much larger than any plane that I had seen before'. The UFO passed overhead from the direction of Stroud and as it did so he detected a sound 'like Rolls Royce turbines of which I believe there were three'. In his letter, passed to MoD by Mr Drew, the observer says 'given this may not be one of ours I wondered if you could look into it... as this is certainly out of the ordinary!' By 2001, when his report was received, the UFO desk did not normally follow-up sightings reported by single witnesses, unless they were members of the armed forces or had some corroborative evidence such as photographs. But on this occasion 'given the resemblance of the diagram... to the "Stealth" aircraft' desk officer Linda Unwin checked with the US Air Force base at RAF Mildenhall in Suffolk. They confirmed there had been 'no unusual US aircraft activity over UK in this period'. DEFE 24/2034/1

David Drew M.P.
House of Commons
Westminster. SW1

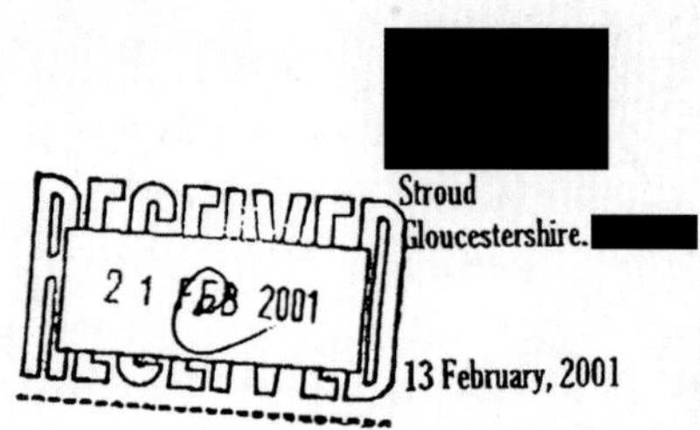

Stroud
Gloucestershire.

21 FEB 2001

13 February, 2001

Dear Mr. Drew,

This is a somewhat unusual question that I would like to ask of you ~ it concerns an aircraft (a very unusual aircraft!), which I saw on the evening of Sunday, September 3rd, 2000. At 9.30pm, when I was out for my usual walk. The place were I saw it was just before passing by the 'Ram' Public House, along 'the Ridge' between Eastcombe and Chalford. — So 8902

As you can imagine, not expecting something like this - it was quite a surprise when I realised what was looming up over the skyline! This was no ordinary aircraft as it was black all over with no tail section that I could determine, and it had three *very* powerful beams of light, lighting up ahead of the aircraft - all three lights emanated from underneath the aircraft from dome-like globes and were set in a triangular shape. The only other lights were extremely small red lights on the extreme tips of each wing, the wing's of which were *extremely* long and much larger than any plane that I had seen before.

The engines were very quite - something like R. Royce turbines of which I believe there were three. The plane passed over me and to my right side heading in the direction of Bisley, but coming from the direction of Stroud/Gloucester approx.

Not alone in my sighting I know of at least one other person who was in Bisley at around the same time, he describes exactly the same sighting as myself.

Given that this may not be one of ours I wondered if you could look into it on my behalf as this is certainly out of the ordinary! I had at that time sent in an initial report about what I had seen to ███████, of Stroud, who records all local UFO sighting's etc. If you have the means to shed some light on this very unusual sighting I would be most grateful for anything that you can find out about it.

Yours sincerely,

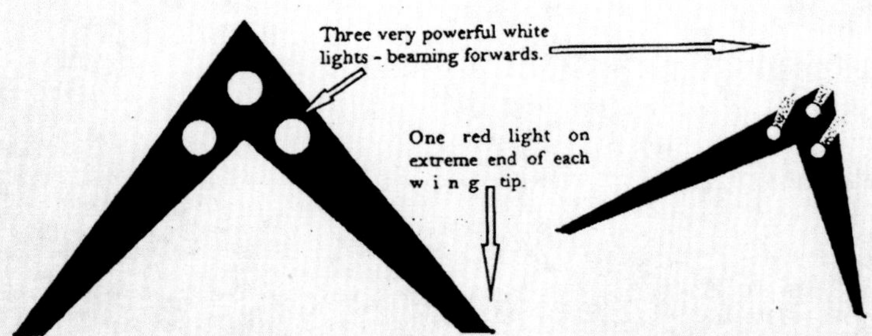

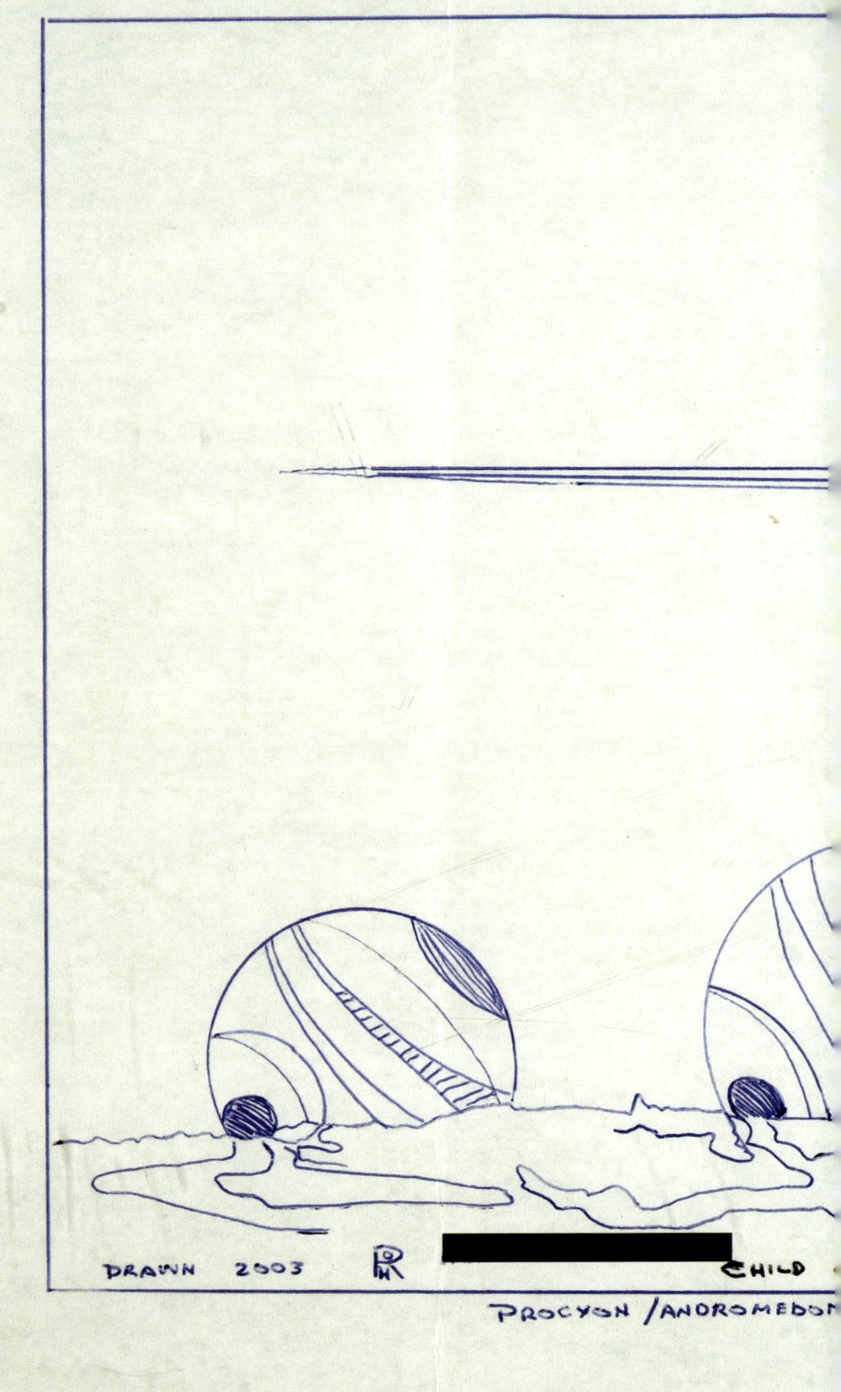

DRAWN 2003
CHILD
PROCYON /ANDROMEDA

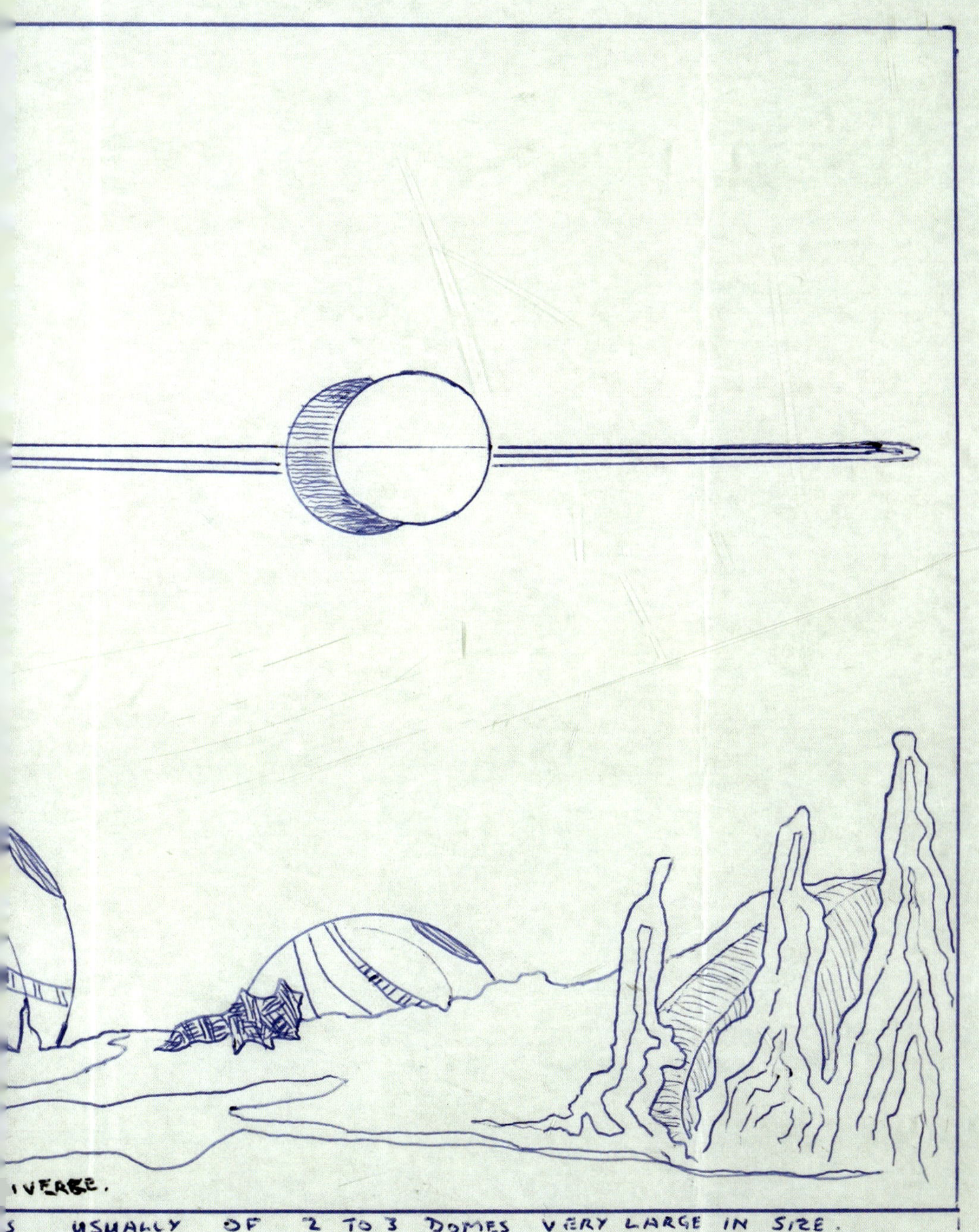

IVERSE.

S USUALLY OF 2 TO 3 DOMES VERY LARGE IN SIZE.
NG 1 MILLION CITYZENS IN EACH. THE DOMES RISE
BEFORE MIDDAY THEY DECEND INTO THE PLANET.
LIKE ACTING AND USING DIFFERENT LANGAUGES WITH
ECT TO EACH OTHER. THEY ARE TELEPATHIC. NOT VERY
L BEINGS.

⟵ *previous spread*

## 2003

Some of the MoD's persistent correspondents claimed to have travelled to alien planets or received telepathic visions of extra-terrestrial cities. In 2003 this drawing of 'what I believe could be the Home World of the Procyons/Andromedons' was sent to the UFO desk by someone who signed themselves as 'Federation Officer' from London. His letter added: 'I suggest we do NOT DESTROY The Procyons/Andromedons, Or Make Any Aggressive Act Againsts Them... As This Could Cause An Ecological Disaster'. DEFE 24/2039/1

*next spread* —▷

## 2004

Occasionally the MoD received reports of UFO phenomena from foreign countries. Among the more striking examples is an account of 'an unusual atmospheric occurrence' observed by an RAF serviceman from the Fylingdales early warning station on the North York Moors. His account was accompanied by two remarkable colour photographs that clearly show what the MoD had begun to classify as a UAP ('unidentified atmospheric phenomenon'). The photographer said that he was on holiday in Habarana in northern Sri Lanka on the afternoon of 27 March 2004 when he 'noticed a partial aura in the sky' that was followed by what sounded like a clap of thunder. Soon afterwards 'a ring like a doughnut' appeared in the sky. It was orange in colour 'with a white/cream colour pushed through... the head of the column glowed an orange colour [and] behind the doughnut was a second cloud of colour and a further ring of orange'. Reporting his experience to MoD on his return to the UK, he added: 'The only way I can describe the sighting is that of an atomic or other type of nuclear explosion, the cloud from which did not rise in the sky, but headed from the high atmosphere towards the earth'. The images resemble what meteorologists classify as an iridescent ice cloud, high in the atmosphere. The cloud appears backlit by the setting sun. But the observer remained convinced he saw 'an air burst of some kind or other'. The MoD decided to take no action and, in response to his report, said: '[this] is a matter for the Sri Lankan government and you may wish to pursue your enquiries with them'. DEFE 24/2036/1

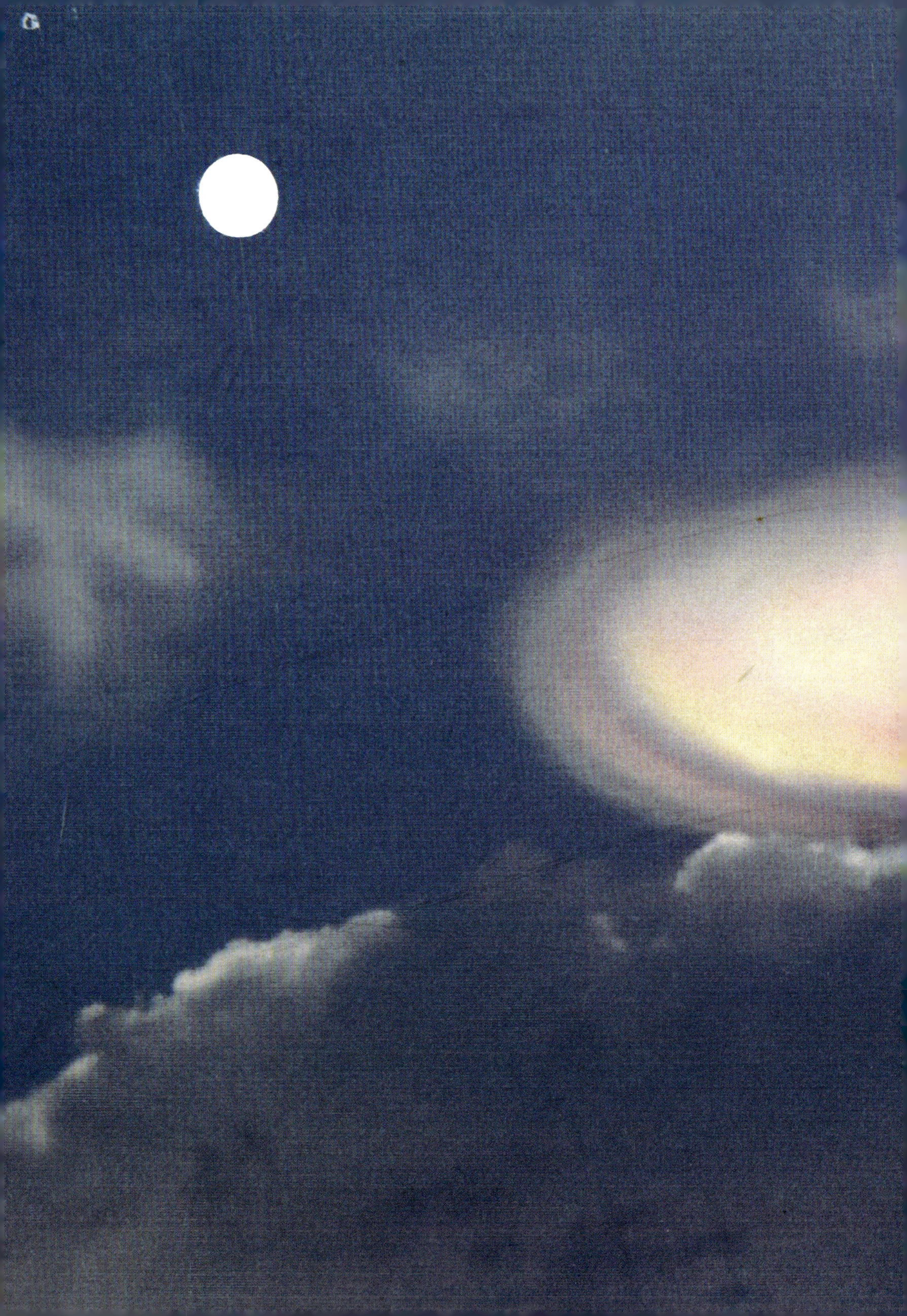

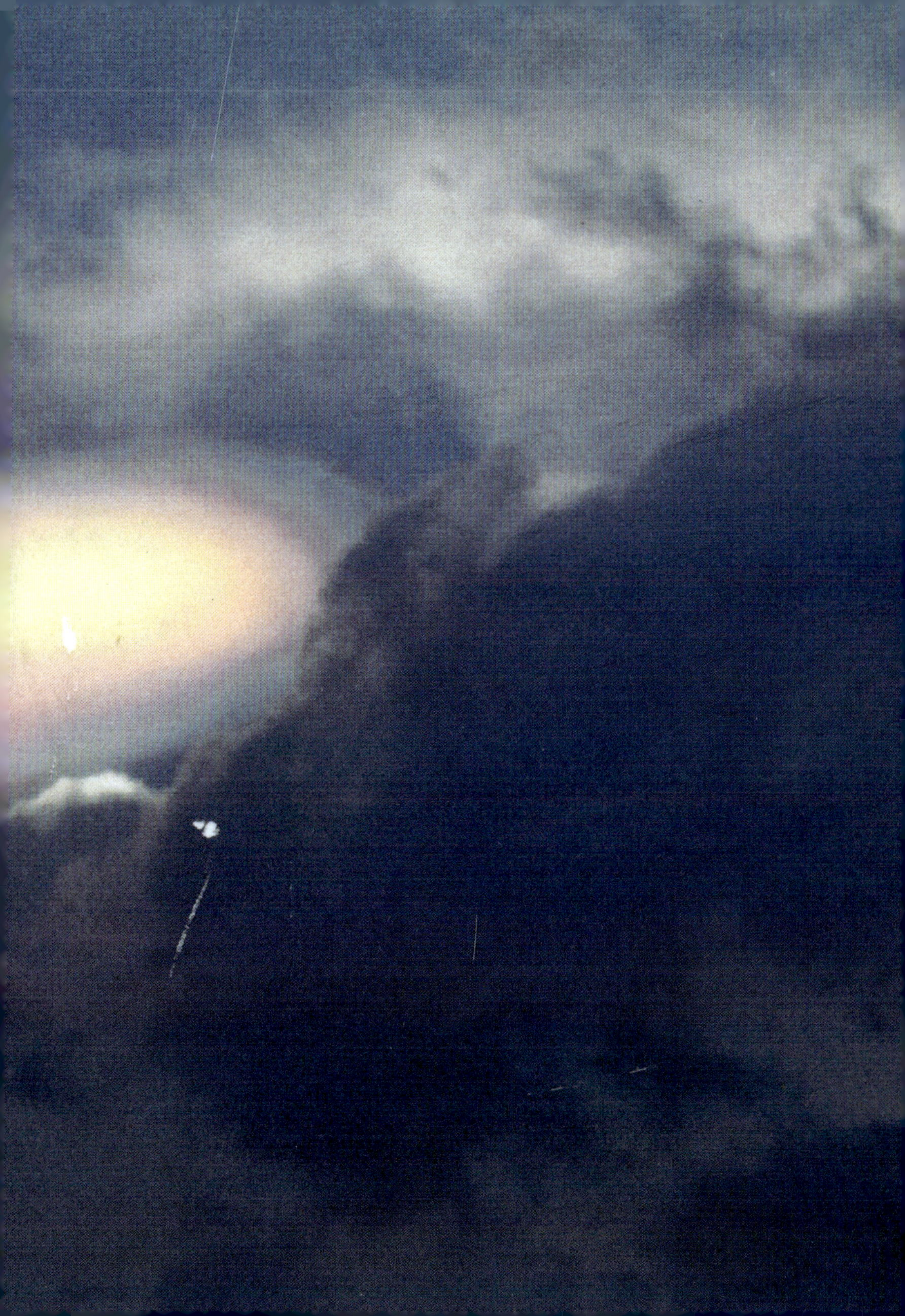

One wintry night in January 2004 Alex Birch took a series of photographs with his Canon 790, using a colour slide film, of the square outside Retford town hall in Nottinghamshire for submission to a photography exhibition. He saw nothing unusual in the sky at the time. But when he examined the transparencies later he was stunned to find an image of a classic flying saucer in the dark sky above the building. Having ruled out lens flares and aircraft he contacted the Ministry of Defence. They said that 'defence experts' would like to take a closer look at the mysterious elliptical object that he had captured on film. Alex personally delivered the slide to the MoD building in London and it was sent to the Defence Geographic and Imagery Intelligence Agency. After computer analysis the DGIA said they were unable to reach any definitive conclusion. Their brief report ends: '...however, it may be coincidental that the illuminated plane of the object passes through the centre of the frame, indicating a possible lens anomaly, e.g. a droplet of water'. Even more bizarre, this was not the first time the Ministry had been left perplexed by a photograph taken by Alex. Back in March 1962, when Alex was a 14-year-old schoolboy, he made news headlines across the world after he took a black and white photograph showing a formation of flying saucers in the sky near his home in Mosborough, Sheffield. The photograph caused such a furore that Alex and his father were invited to visit Whitehall, where both the image and his Box Brownie camera were examined by Air Ministry experts. In a letter the ministry told Alex's father '...the photograph can be explained in mundane terms and does not mean that so-called unidentified flying objects must have been over Sheffield at the time it was taken'. Eight years later Alex confessed he had faked the image by painting the saucers onto a sheet of glass that he photographed. 'It was just unbelievable that everyone was taken in by it,' he told the *Sheffield Telegraph*. But in an amazing turnaround, twenty-five years later in 1997, following the 50th anniversary of the UFO mystery, Alex claimed his hoax confession was itself a hoax. He said he had made the announcement to avoid unwelcome media attention – and the photograph was genuine after all, adding that the Roswell Museum in New Mexico wanted his old Box Brownie to put on display, but he wished to keep it. 'It seems that one black and white picture taken in a garden all those years ago will be having an impact on our lives for some years to come'. AIR 2/16918; DEFE 24/2060/1

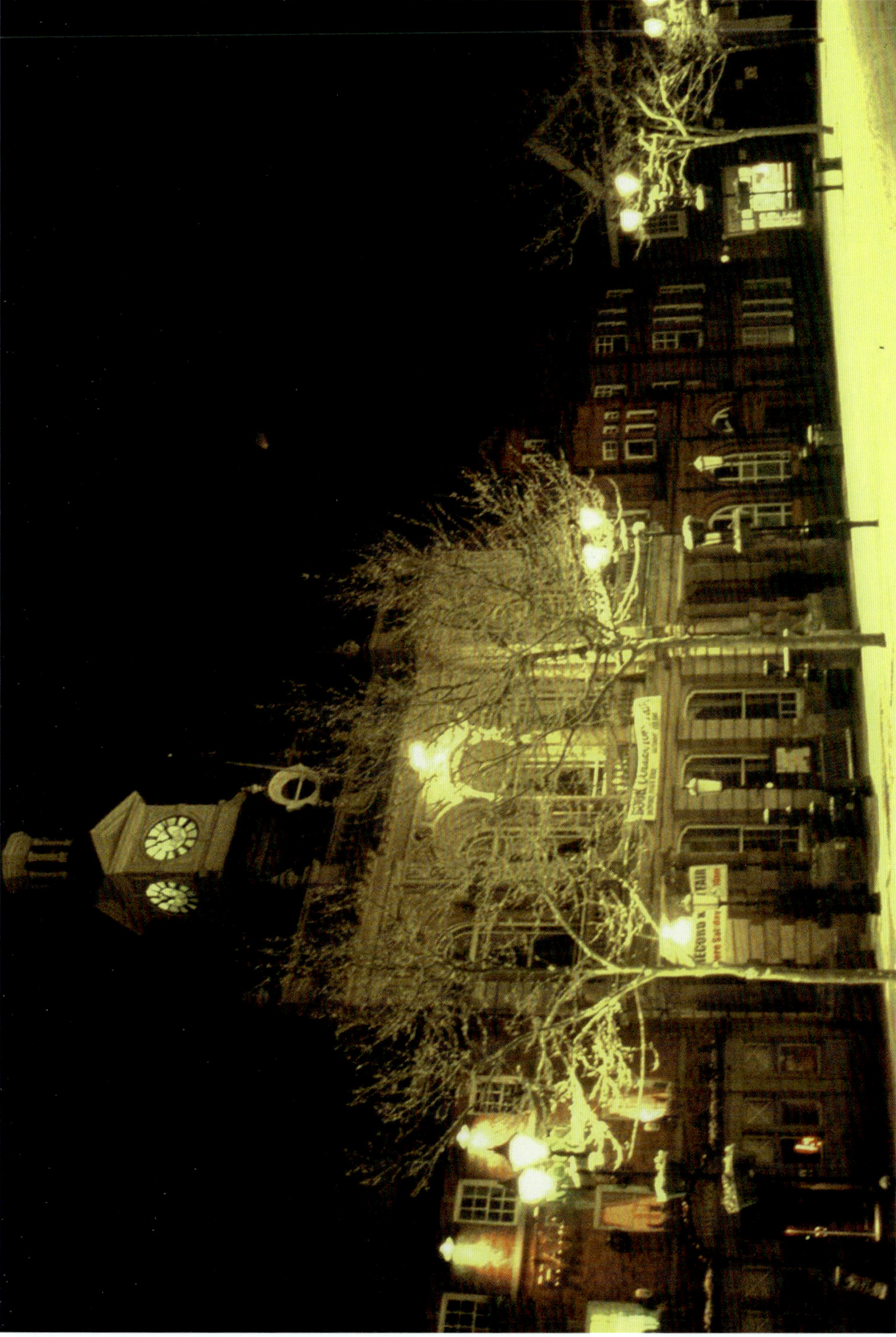

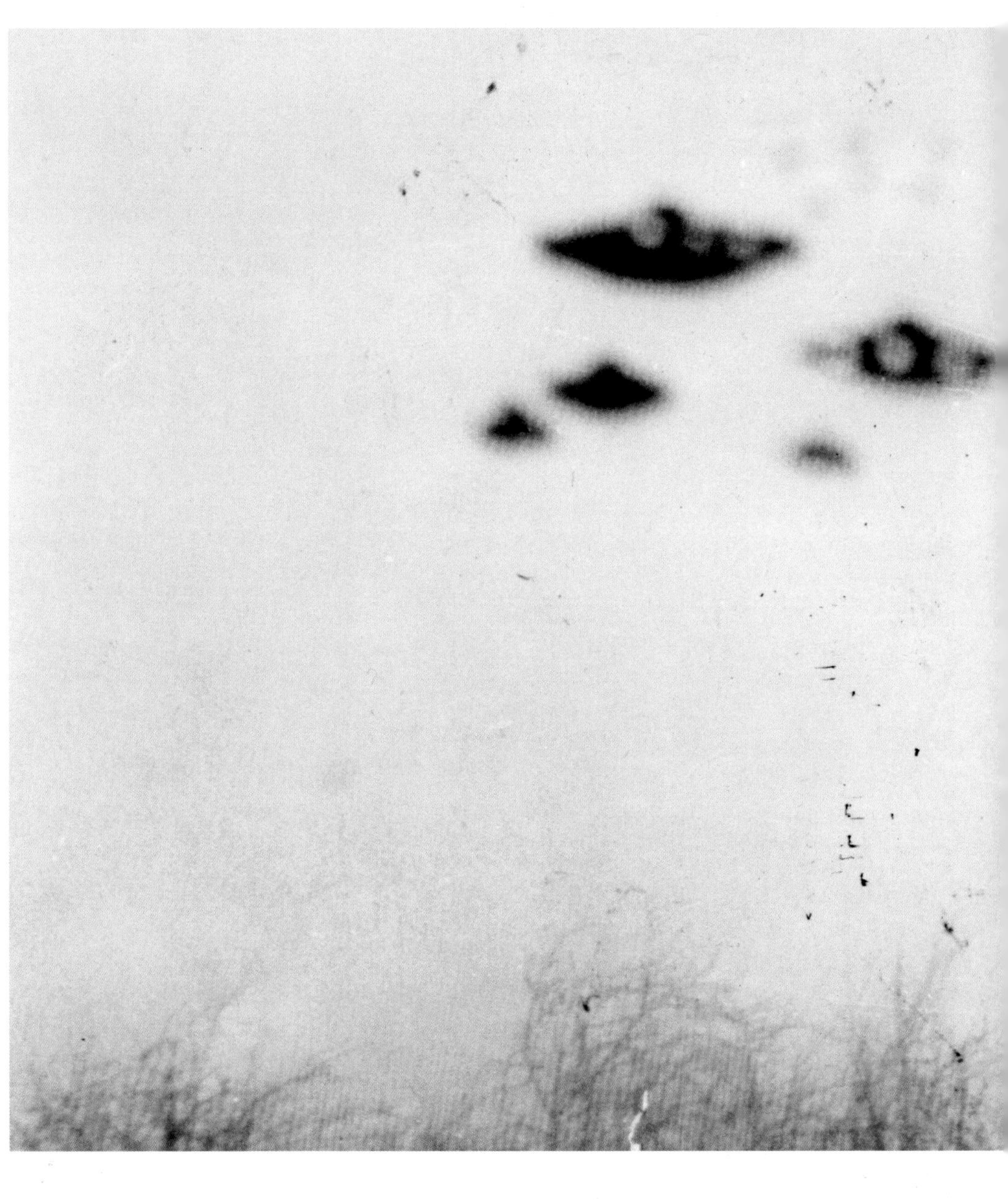

The National Archives is the official archive and publisher for the UK Government, and for England and Wales. It works to bring together and secure the future of the public record, both digital and physical, for future generations.

The National Archives is open to all, offering a range of activities and spaces to enjoy, as well as reading rooms for research. Many of the most popular records are also available online.

nationalarchives.gov.uk

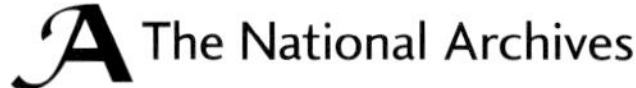 The National Archives

RESTRICTED/UNCLASSIFIED

M.O.D. Form 48D

# MINISTRY OF DEFENCE

## PART IV

1. ATTENTION IS DRAWN TO THE NOTES ON THE INSIDE FLAP

2. ENTER NOTES OF RELATED FILES ON PAGE 2 OF THIS JACKET

**DIVISION**

FOR REGISTRY USE ONLY

**1996**

Registered file number

**AF/ 7463/72 PART IV**

Date opened
24 - 6 - 71

DOWNGRADED & RE-REG FROM AF/CX 38/67 PT VII

M.O.D.
ID/47/274
A.H.B. (RAF) (Pt.4)

**SUBJECT**

UNIDENTIFIED FLYING OBJECTS - REPORTS.

| Referred to | DATE | Referred to | DATE | Referred to | DATE | DATE |
|---|---|---|---|---|---|---|
| S4 f (AIR) | 9 - 11 - 72 | | | | | |
| S4 f (AIR) | 9 - 11 - 72 | | | | | |

CLOSED

NO FURTHER MINUTES OR ENCLOSURES MUST BE PLACED IN THIS FILE

AIR 20/12399

CLOSED UNTIL 2003

S 1889

DATE FOR 1996

(a) SECOND REVIEW

(b) DESTRUCTION

REVIEWED BY.
DRO (AIR AND CENTRE) M.O.D.

DISPO

DOWNGRADING
(to be completed when the file goes out of current use)

...ded to UNCLASSIFIED on
(Insert date)

APPOINTMENT AND BRANCH

OR
(ii) Return for review on (Insert date)

**RESTRICTED/UNCLASSIFIE**

(9815) D. 540177 102m (4 sorts) 8/71 F.J. Gp. 610

# RESTRICTED OR
# UNCLASSIFIED

PRO
ON 18/8/94 S

M.O.D.
I_D/48/84
A.H.B. (RAF)

## MINISTRY OF DEFENCE
## BRANCH FOLDER

1

NUMBER

**AF** S4f (AIR) 527

AIR 20/12058

DATE OPENED 1-4-69

DIVISION/DIRECTORATE/BRANCH:

S4f (AIR)
083752

REGISTERED
FILE NUMBER:

SUBJECT:

U.F.Os APRIL 1969

527

**CLOSED UNTIL 2000**

| Referred | Date |
| --- | --- |
| | |

TO BE RET... ...e UNTIL
1999) IN A... ...PUBLIC

1.  The conten... ...r
    items on a...

2.  Branch Fold... ...n
    directorate, or branch.  They are not to be sent to other
    divisions or directorates.  Their movements are NOT recorded
    by the Registry.

(5393) D. 377662 20m 2/68 P.I. Gp. 610

Four Corners Books is an independent publisher based in London. Our series,
Four Corners Irregulars, presents a visual history of modern British culture.

Titles include:
1. Eyeball Cards, The Art Of British CB Radio Culture
2. UFO Drawings From The National Archives
3. Poster Workshop 1968–1971
4. Leeds Postcards
5. Face In The Crowd
6. Wobbly Sounds, A Collection Of British Flexidiscs
7. Nuclear War In The UK
8. Women For Peace: Banners From Greenham Common
   ...with further volumes in preparation.

fourcornersbooks.co.uk

*Four Corners Irregulars*
A series of books about modern British
visual culture. This is book 2.

The publisher would like to thank all those
at The National Archives who worked on
this project and helped to make it possible.

Set in Starling and printed
on Garda Matt Art Ultra.

Published in 2017 by Four Corners Books
56 Artillery Lane, London E1 7LS

Designed by John Morgan studio
morganstudio.co.uk

Print production by Martin Lee
Reprography by Martin Chapman
Printed in Italy by Printer Trento
Fourth printing 2025

Distributed in the UK by Art Data
artdata.co.uk

ISBN 978-1-909829-09-1

Observe us in cyberspace at
fourcornersbooks.co.uk